THIS BOOK BELONGS TO:

_____

A Children's Treasury of Milligan

A Children's Treasury of Milligan

CLASSIC STORIES
& POEMS

by

Spike Milligan

Virgin

First published in this form in 2000 by
Virgin Publishing Limited
Thames Wharf Studios
Rainville Road
London
W6 9HA.

First Published in Great Britain 1999

ISBN 1 85227 970 2

A catalogue record for this book is available from the British Library.

Designed by Design 23, London.
Spike Milligan's original illustrations were hand coloured by Ron Callow at Design 23.
Colour Reproduction by Colourwise Ltd.
Printed and bound in Great Britain by Bath Press.

CONTENTS

INTRODUCTION

Amazing news! After searching the world they managed to get together six separate books of mine: one was found in a haddock-stretching factory; another was found in a dead whale in Newfoundland; another was found in the back pocket of my trousers; another one was found by a diver 500 feet down in the Irish Sea; another was found in an elephant's trunk in Zambia and the sixth one was just found.

So I wish you well and, at 81 years of age, I hope you wish me well.

1998 was a wonderful year for me. My poem 'On The Ning Nang Nong' was voted the Nation's Favourite Comic Poem – now will they give me a knighthood?

SPIKE MILLIGAN, 1999

Silly Verse for Kids

CONTENTS

FOREWORD

Most of these poems were written to amuse
my children; some were written as a result of
things they said in the home. No matter what
you say, my kids think I'm brilliant!

S.M.

Look at all those monkeys

Look at all those monkeys
Jumping in their cage.
Why don't they all go out to work
And earn a decent wage?

How can you say such silly things,
Are you a son of mine?
Imagine monkeys travelling on
The Morden-Edgware line!

But what about the Pekinese!
They have an allocation.
'Don't travel during Peke hour,'
It says on every station.

My Gosh, you're right, my clever boy,
I never thought of that!
And so they left the monkey house,
While an elephant raised his hat.

String

String
Is a very important thing.
Rope is thicker,
But string,
Is quicker.

P.S. The meaning of this is obscure
    That's why, the higher the fewer.

Mary Pugh

Mary Pugh
Was nearly two
When she went out of doors.
She went out standing up she did
But came back on all fours.
The moral of the story
Please meditate and pause:
Never send a baby out
With loosely waisted draws.

Tell me little woodworm

Tell me little woodworm
Eating thru the wood.
Surely all that sawdust
Can't do you any good.

Heavens! Little woodworm
You've eaten all the chairs
So *that's* why poor old Grandad's
Sitting outside on the stairs.

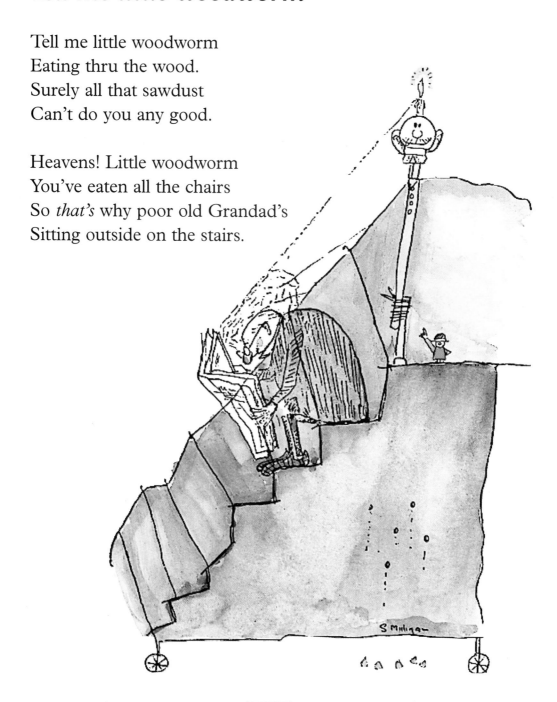

Hipporhinostricow

Such a beast is the Hipporhinostricow
How it got so mixed up we'll never know how;
It sleeps all day, and whistles all night,
And it wears yellow socks which are far too tight.

If you laugh at the Hipporhinostricow,
You're bound to get into an awful row;
The creature is protected you see
From silly people like you and me.

I've never felt finer

'I've never felt finer!'
Said the King of China,
Sitting down to dine –
Then fell down dead – he died he did!
It was only half past nine.

Said the General

Said the General of the Army,
'I think that war is barmy'
So he threw away his gun:
Now he's having much more fun.

Two children (small)

Two children (small), one Four, one Five,
Once saw a bee go in a hive.
They'd never seen a bee before!
So waited there to see some more.
And sure enough along there came
A dozen bees (and all the same!)
Within the hive they buzzed about;
Then, one by one, they all flew *out*.
Said Four: 'Those bees *are* silly things,
But *how* I *wish* I *had* their *wings*!'

Granny

Through every nook and every cranny
The wind blew in on poor old Granny;
Around her knees, into each ear
(And up her nose as well, I fear).

All through the night the wind grew worse,
It nearly made the vicar curse.
The top had fallen off the steeple
Just missing him (and other people).

It blew on man, it blew on beast.
It blew on nun, it blew on priest.
It blew the wig off Auntie Fanny –
But most of all, it blew on Granny ! !

Hello Jolly Guardsman

'Hello Jolly Guardsman
In your scarlet coat:
It reaches from below your tum
To half way up your throat.'

'Tell me Jolly Guardsman
When you're off parade
What kind of clothes do you put on?'
'Civvies I'm afraid.'

Today I saw a little worm

Today I saw a little worm
Wriggling on his belly.
Perhaps he'd like to come inside
And see what's on the Telly.

Teeth

English Teeth, English Teeth!
Shining in the sun
A part of British heritage
Aye, each and every one.

English Teeth, Happy Teeth!
Always having fun
Clamping down on bits of fish
And sausages half done.

English Teeth! HEROES' Teeth!
Hear then click! and clack!
Let's sing a song of praise to them –
Three Cheers for the Brown Grey
and Black.

Can a parrot

Can a parrot
Eat a carrot
Standing on his head?
If I did that my mum would
   send me
Straight upstairs to bed.

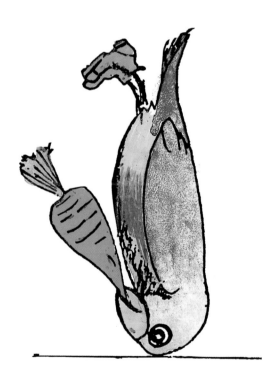

I'm not frightened of Pussy Cats

I'm not frightened of Pussy Cats
They only eat up mice and rats,
But a Hippopotamus
Could eat the Lotofus!

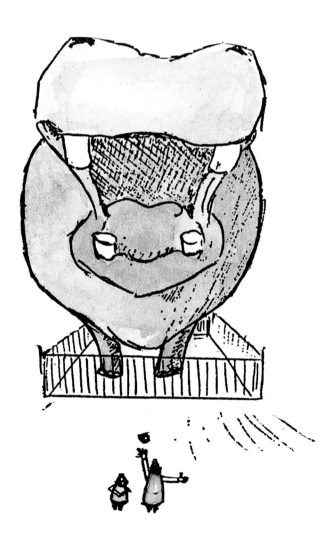

Down the stream the swans all glide

Down the stream the swans all glide;
It's quite the cheapest way to ride.
Their legs get wet,
Their tummies wetter:
I think after all
The bus is better.

On the Ning Nang Nong

On the Ning Nang Nong
Where the Cows go Bong!
And the Monkeys all say Boo!
There's a Nong Nang Ning
Where the trees go Ping!
And the tea pots Jibber Jabber Joo.

On the Nong Ning Nang
All the mice go Clang!
And you just can't catch 'em when they do!
So it's Ning Nang Nong!
Cows go Bong!
Nong Nang Ning!
Trees go Ping!
Nong Ning Nang!
The mice go Clang!
What a noisy place to belong,
Is the Ning Nang
   Ning Nang Nong! !

The Land of the Bumbley Boo

In the Land of the Bumbley Boo
The people are red white and blue,
They never blow noses,
Or ever wear closes,
What a sensible thing to do!

In the Land of the Bumbley Boo
You can buy Lemon pie at the Zoo;
They give away Foxes
In little Pink Boxes
And Bottles of Dandylion Stew.

In the Land of the Bumbley Boo
You never see a Gnu,
But thousands of cats
Wearing trousers and hats
Made of Pumpkins and Pelican Glue!

Chorus
Oh, the Bumbley Boo! the Bumbley Boo!
That's the place for me and you!
So hurry! Let's run!
The train leaves at one!
For the Land of the Bumbley Boo!
The wonderful Bumbley Boo-Boo-Boo!
The Wonderful Bumbley BOO!!!

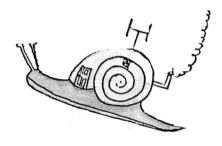

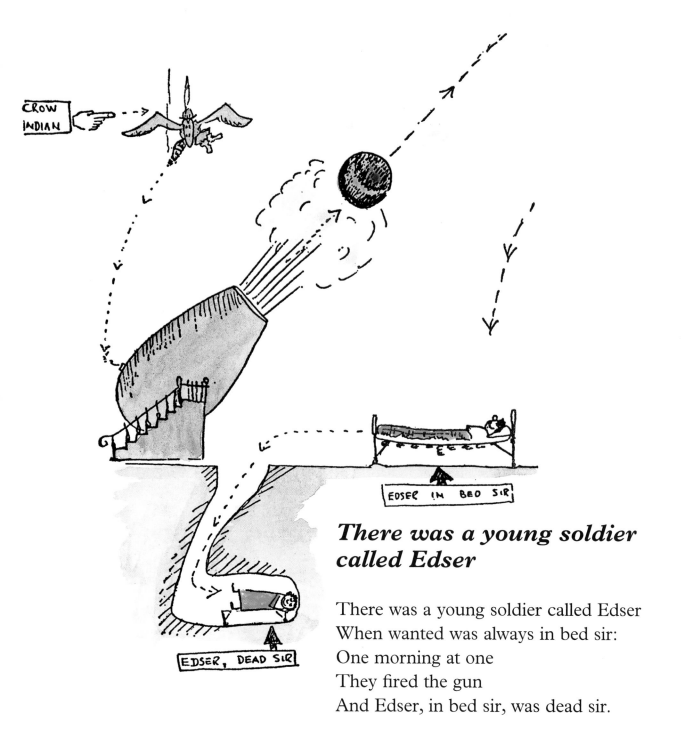

CROW INDIAN

EDSER IN BED SIR

EDSER, DEAD SIR

There was a young soldier called Edser

There was a young soldier called Edser
When wanted was always in bed sir:
One morning at one
They fired the gun
And Edser, in bed sir, was dead sir.

You must never bath in an Irish Stew

You must never bath in an Irish Stew
It's a most illogical thing to do
But should you persist against
   my reasoning
Don't fail to add the appropriate
   seasoning.

Hello Mr Python

Hello Mr Python
Curling round a tree
Bet you'd like to make yourself
A dinner out of me.

Can't you change your habits
Crushing people's bones?
I wouldn't like a dinner
That emitted fearful groans.

Failure

I'm trying to write the longest first line that poetry has ever had,
For a start that wasn't bad,
Now here comes a longer
oneeeeeeeeeeeeeeeeeeeeeeeeeeeeeeeeeeeeeeee
I know I cheated:
It was the only way I could avoid being defeated.

My sister Laura

My sister Laura's bigger than me
And lifts me up quite easily.
I can't lift her, I've tried and tried;
She must have something heavy inside.

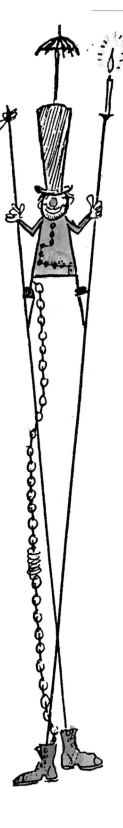

The Bongaloo

'What is a Bongaloo, Daddy?'
'A Bongaloo, Son,' said I,
'Is a tall bag of cheese
Plus a Chinaman's knees
And the leg of a nanny goat's eye.'

'How strange is a Bongaloo, Daddy?'
'As strange as strange,' I replied.
'When the sun's in the West
It appears in a vest
Sailing out with the noonday tide.'

'What shape is a Bongaloo, Daddy?'
'The shape, my Son, I'll explain:
It's tall round the nose
Which continually grows
In the general direction of Spain.'

'Are you *sure* there's a Bongaloo,
    Daddy?'
'Am I sure, my Son?' said I.
'Why, I've seen it, not quite
On a dark sunny night
Do you think that I'd tell you a lie?'

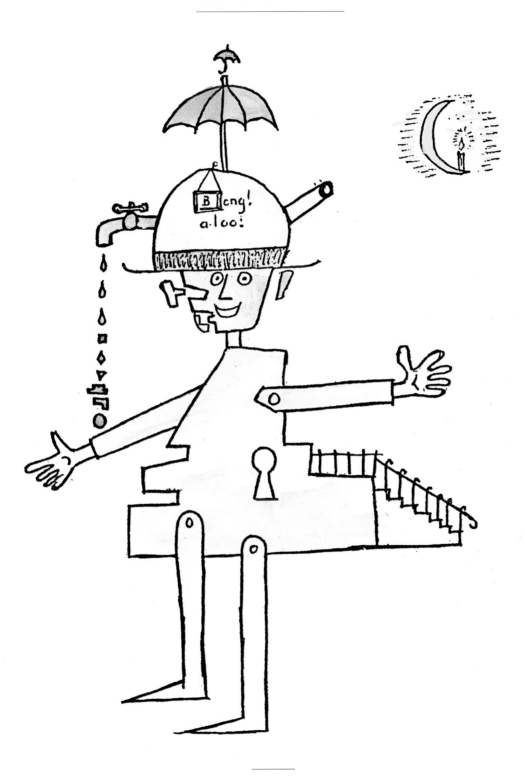

I once knew a Burmese horse

I once knew a Burmese horse:
Of course
He didn't know he was a horse;
But I knew Jim
So I told him –
Now he knows
And so, I close.

My daddy wears a big black hat

My daddy wears a big black hat;
He wears it in the street
And raises it to lady folk
That he perchance should meet.
He wears it on a Sunday
And on a Monday too.
He never wears it in the house,
But only out of doors.

Maveric

Maveric Prowles
Had Rumbling Bowels
That thundered in the night.
It shook the bedrooms all around
And gave the folks a fright.

The doctor called;
He was appaled
When through his stethoscope
He heard the sound of a baying
    hound,
And the acrid smell of smoke.

Was there a cure?
'The higher the fewer,'
The learned doctor said,
Then turned poor Maveric
    inside out
And stood him on his head.

'Just as I thought
You've been and caught
An Asiatic flu –
You mustn't go near dogs I fear
Unless they come near you.'

Poor Maveric cried.
He went cross-eyed,
His legs went green and blue.
The doctor hit him with a club
And charged him one and two.

And so my friend
This is the end,
A warning to the few:
Stay clear of doctors to the end
Or they'll get rid of you.

Contagion

Elephants are contagious!
Be careful how you tread.
An Elephant that's been trodden on
Should be confined to bed!

Leopards are contagious too.
Be careful tiny tots.
They don't give you a temperature
But lots and lots – of spots.

The Herring is a lucky fish,
From all disease inured.
Should he be ill when caught at sea:
Immediately – he's cured!

Round and Round

Small poem based upon my daughter's (6) remarks on overhearing me tell her brother Sean (4½) that the world was going round. (Australia, June-July, 1958.)

One day a little boy called Sean
(Age four) became profound.
He asked his dad
If it were true
The world was going round.

'Oh yes, that's true,' his daddy said.
'It goes round night and day.'
'Then doesn't it get tired dad?'
Young Sean was heard to say.

His sister in the bath called out
'What did dad say – what did he?'
He said 'The world is going round.'
Said she 'Well it's making me giddy!'

Soldier Freddy

Soldier Freddy was never ready
But Soldier Neddy,
  unlike Freddy
Was <u>always</u> ready and steady.

That's why,
When soldier Neddy
Is-outside-Buckingham-Palace-
on-guard-in-the-pouring-wind-
and-rain-being-steady-and-
ready,
Freddie – is home in beddy.

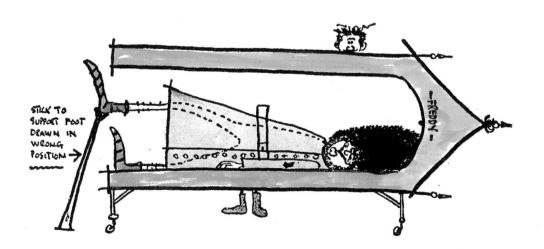

The ABC

T'was midnight in the schoolroom
And every desk was shut,
When suddenly from the alphabet
Was heard a loud 'Tut-tut!'

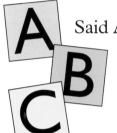

Said A to B, 'I don't like C;
His manners are a lack.
For all I ever see of C
Is a semi-circular back!'

'I disagree,' said D to B,
'I've never found C so.
From where I stand,
he seems to be
An uncompleted O.'

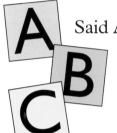

C was vexed, 'I'm much perplexed,
You criticize my shape.
I'm made like that, to help spell Cat
and Cow and Cool and Cape.'

'He's right,' said E; said F,
'Whoopee!'
Said G, ' 'Ip, 'ip, 'ooray!'
'You're dropping me,' roared H to G.
'Don't do it please I pray!'

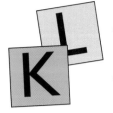

'Out of my way,'
LL said to K.
'I'll make poor I
look ILL.
To stop this stunt,
J stood in front,
And presto! ILL was JILL.

'U know,' and V, 'that W
Is twice the age of me,
From as a Roman V is five
I'm half as young
as he.'

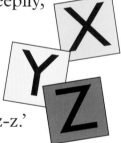

X and Y yawned sleepily,
'Look at the time!'
they said.
'Let's all get off to
beddy byes.'
They did, then 'Z-z-z.'

or

alternative last verse

X and Y yawned sleepily,
'Look at the time!' they said.
They all jumped in to beddy
byes
And the last one in was Z!

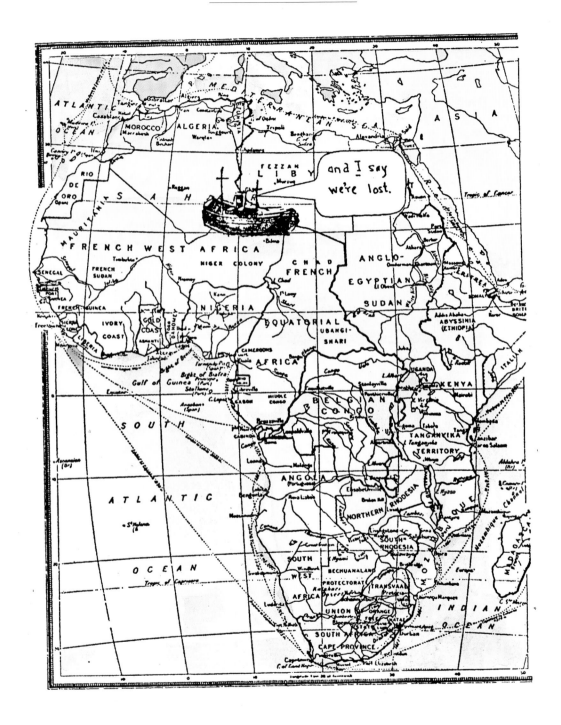

Bump!

Things that go 'bump!' in the night,
Should not really give one a fright.
It's the hole in each ear
That lets in the fear,
That, and the absence of light!

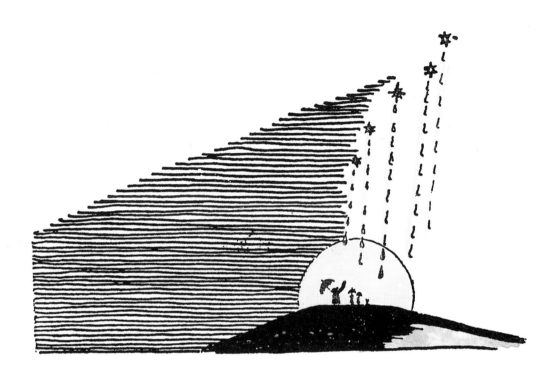

Rain

There are holes in the sky
Where the rain gets in,
But they're every so small
That's why rain is thin.

A
Book
of

Milliganimals

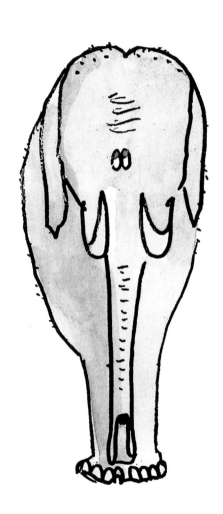

CONTENTS

PART ONE

ANIMALS

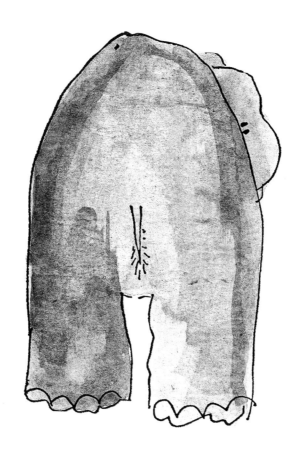

HIP-HIP-HIPPO!

THREE LEGGED HIPPO

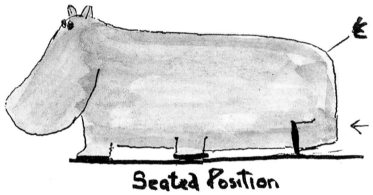

Seated Position

RARE BACK
VIEW

Arctic Elephant

Arctic Elephants are the same as African ones only they're colder. Feel one.

Moos

Highly trained Moo-Cows doing impressions★ of Moo-Zebras.

★ First impression 1968

Strawberry Moose

Leopards

Leopards are easily spotted.
Just fill in the white circles with
black ink.

The Cheetah

A sleek cat is the Cheetah,
No other could look neetah,
He's heavily dotted ...
So he's easily spotted ...
And he lives in Tanganyika.

Pygmy Elephant

The Pygmy Elephant is made
Much shorter than the giant brigade.
He lives much closer to the ground
And that is where he's usually found.
Why should an Elephant be so wee?
My friend, it's no good asking *me*!

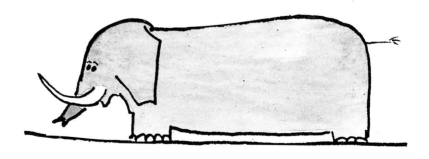

Alligator

From Sydney Zoo
An Alligator
Was put on board
A flying freighter.
He ate the pilot
And the navigator
Then asked for more,
With mashed potater.

Much later

Tiger, Tiger Burning etc

Tigers travel stealthily
Using, first, legs one and three.
They alternate with two and four;
And, after that, there are no more.

Envoi
Tiger, tiger burning bright,
Look out! You'll set the jungle alight.

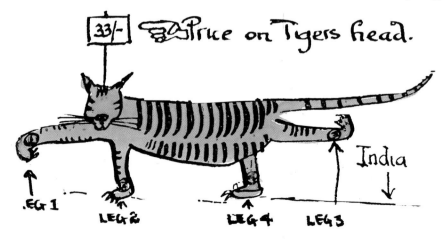

Ant and Eleph-Ant

Said a tiny Ant
To the Elephant,
'Mind how you tread in this
clearing!'

But alas! Cruel fate!
She was crushed by the weight
Of an Elephant, hard of hearing.

EX-SERVICE ANT.
WIFE, 3 CHILDREN
AND ELEPHANTS LEG
TO SUPPORT.

Silly Old Baboon

There was a Babooon
Who, one afternoon,
Said, 'I think I will fly to the sun.'
So, with two great palms
Strapped to his arms,
He started his take-off run.

Mile after mile
He galloped in style
But never once left the ground.
'You're running too slow,'
Said a passing crow,
'Try reaching the speed of sound.'

So he put on a spurt –
By God how it hurt!
The soles of his feet caught fire.
There were great clouds of steam
As he raced through a stream
But he still didn't get any higher.

Racing on through the night,
Both his knees caught alight
And smoke billowed out from his
    rear.
Quick to his aid
Came a fire brigade
Who chased him for over a year.

Many moons passed by.
Did Baboon ever fly?
Did he ever get to the sun?
I've just heard today
That he's well on his way!
He'll be passing through Acton
    at one.

P.S. Well, what do you expect from a
Baboon?

The Lion

A Lion is fierce:
His teeth can pierce
The skin of a postman's knee.

It serves him right
That, because of his bite,
He gets no letters you see.

The Pig

A very rash young lady pig
(They say she was a smasher)
        Suddenly ran
        Under a van –
Now she's a gammon rasher.

Giraffe no. 1

We come now to
the stately Giraffe
Who's never been known
to smile or laugh.

But once, long ago,
he laughed at a Tory
Who told him, they say,
a very tall story!

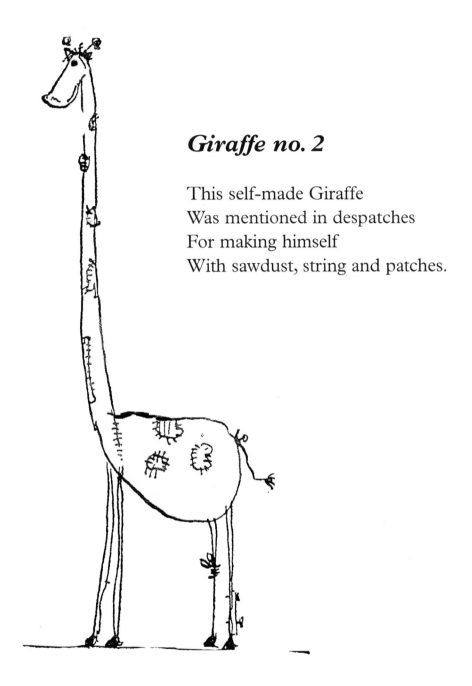

Giraffe no. 2

This self-made Giraffe
Was mentioned in despatches
For making himself
With sawdust, string and patches.

PART TWO

Milliganimals

Fish

A tourist who went to Tunisia
Said, 'Are we allowed to go fishing 'ere?'
        'Oh no,' said the Bey.
        'All the fish gone away.
I've only got chips on my dish in 'ere.'

Sardines

A baby Sardine
Saw her first submarine:
She was scared and watched through a peephole.

'Oh, come, come, come,'
Said the Sardine's mum,
'It's only a tin full of people.'

The Admiral Byrd

You must have heard
Of the Admiral Byrd
Who found a pole called South.

He flew *all* the way
From the USA!
Well Lawdy hush ma mouth!

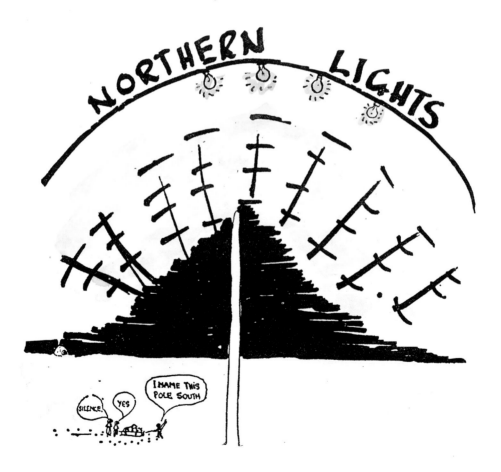

Onecan   Toucans

The Gofongo

The Gofongo, if you please,
Is a fish with singing knees
And a tail that plays
The Spanish clarinet!

He has toes that whistle tunes
And explode! Like toy balloons.
Hence his many,
Many visits to the vet.

The Gofongo, when he likes,
Swallows jam and rusty bikes,
Orange pips and treacle
Pudding boiled in glue.

He loves chips with rusty nails
And can swallow *iron rails*
That is why they cannot
Keep one in a zoo.

But! Gofongo as a pet
Would cause panic and regret.
People tried it and were
Nearly driven balmy.

For, once inside a house,
He screams, 'I'm a Jewish mouse.'
Then he runs away –
And joins the Arab Army!

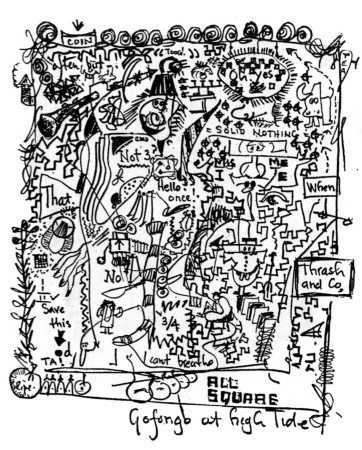

The Flea

How teeny teeny wee
Is the little tiny flea.
One would think that one so small
Could do no harm at all.
But all last night
In my hotel
He made me scratch
Like merry hell.

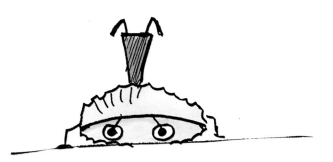

Wiggle-Woggle

The Wiggle-Woggle said,
'When I'm standing on my head
I can see the coast of China
And it's very, very Red.'

Words Said

'Bunga-louie lee!'
Said the monkey to the flea.
It wasn't much to say *but* –
It passed the time away.

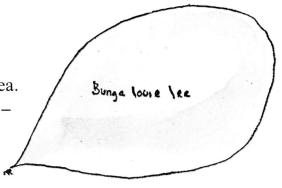

'Bunga-louie-lee.' Word invented
by Silé when popping a hand
puppet around my bedroom door.
She was about seven at the time.

What the Wiggle-Woggle said

The Wiggle-Woggle said,
'I wish that I were dead:
I've a pain in my tummy and
It's travelling up the bed.
I wish that I were something
That never got a pain;
A little bit of fluffy stuff
That vanished down the drain.
I could be a tiger's whisker,
A tuba made of bread,
The purple eye
Of a custard pie
With a trouser made of lead.
There *must* be other somethings –
A tiny leather bead?
Or a bit of crumpled paper
Where the water-melons feed?
A yellow thing with lumps on!
A yellow thing without!!
Some hairy stuff
On a powder puff
That snuffs the candles out.
Wish I were a lamp post

(Lamp posts don't get pains),
A leaky rusty gutter
Flooding other people's drains!
All *those* are what I'd like to be,'
The Wiggle-Woggle said.

But he stayed a Wiggle-Woggle
And, what's more, he stayed in bed!

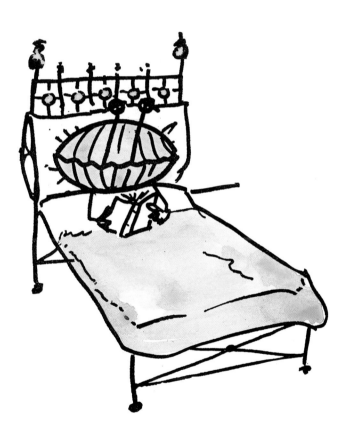

The sad happy ending story of

The
Bald Twit
Lion

A story for very all ages

Monkey involved in Bald Twit Lion story.
Also cashier at Chester Zoo.

Once, twice and thrice upon a time there lived a Jungle. It started at the bottom and went upwards till it reached the monkeys, who had been waiting years for the trees to reach them, and as soon as they did the monkeys invented climbing down. Most trees were made of wood, and so were the rest. Trees never spoke, not even to each other, so they never said much (actually one tree did once say 'much' but nobody believed him), they never said 'fish' either, not even on Fridays. It was a really good Jungle: great scarlet lilies, yellow irises, thousands of grasses all grew very happily, and this Jungle was always on time. Some people are always late, like the late King George V. But not this Jungle.

This Jungle became very, very popular with lots of wonderful animals; there was absolutely no shortage of them and therefore the Jungle was ever so busy. This Jungle was called the Bozzollika-Dowser Jungle. Because. There was no organization there, but *everything* worked out perfectly. Some scientists tried to make an organized Jungle of plastic, but it didn't improve conditions and the scientists left saying, 'Let's go to the moon instead,' and as there is nothing on the moon it seemed the best place for them. Men kept coming to the Jungle looking for gold, diamonds, gas and oil. Whereas simple animals could live without the things, brilliant man couldn't, in fact he'd forgotten how to. One thing he never forgot was how to have wars and say, 'Oh dear, how sad,' when children were killed by bombs. The animals left these things called men alone. In return for this kindness man killed them, cut off their skins and put them on the floor, cut their heads off and stuck them on the walls. But if ever an animal killed a man, it was in *all* the newspapers.

But this story is a hap-hap-happy story, about animals. One day in the middle of the Jungle, near a village called Pongoland, a big lion called Mr Gronk had an attack of strongness. He was twenty-one that day and had been given the key to the Jungle, so he put on a fierce look and then, leaping in the air, he gave the biggest, loudest roar in the world. **'ROAR – ROAR ROAR!! ROAR!!!'** he went; in fact he roared so loud that it loosened all the roots of his hair and tinkle tinkle all this lovely mane fell off, and landed on the ground PLIP-PLAP-PLOP 200,000 times, one for every hair. Suddenly Mr Gronk the lion saw himself in the *Daily Mirror* and, oh! he saw that he was now bald! A *Bald* Lion? 'Oh dearie me, I'll be the laughing stock of the hyenas,' he said. So he un-roared, **'!ЯОАЯ !ЯОАЯ !ЯОАЯ',** but his hairs didn't go back in, they just lay there smiling up at him, in hairy (that's hair language). Poor Mr Gronk,

He roared so load it loosened all the roots of his hairs and they fell out.

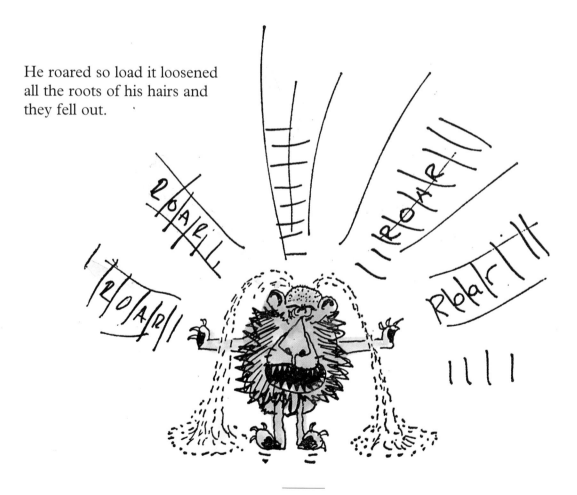

One-legged Bald Twit Lion.

he now looked like a bald twit lion. As a passing hippopotamus said, 'I am a passing hippopotamus,' and went on to say, 'you look like a bald hairless twit lion.' When the lion heard that, he became naughty, angry and was just about to do a BIG roar, but no! he stopped, *just* in time; he'd better not roar any more, or something else might drop off him! He would look even sillier as a one-legged bald hairless twit lion, so, from then on when he was angry, he could only say very quietly, 'Tsu-tsu-tsu,' and there is nothing funnier that a bald hairless twit lion called Mr Gronk leaping about the Jungle going, 'Tsu-tsu-tsu'.

One night when he was having tea (Lyons) he said, 'I can't go on being bald. It's a big problem: I must find a solution.' So he squeezed every tube in the Jungle but not one had the right solution in it. Then he thought, 'I'll try straining very hard and think about growing hairs.' So he strained, *strained* and STRAINED, but it only made his eyes water and his

inches 3

inches 4

Bald Twit Lion leaping and saying, 'Tsu! Tsu!'

nose bleed. Everyone laughed. His own flea left him. 'There's nowhere to hide on a bald twit lion,' he said and hopped it. He bribed a part-time hairy anteater to sit on his head; it really looked like real hair, but the lion got hiccups and, each time, hairy anteater fell off. 'I'm off,' he said (which was obvious as he'd just fallen off). Lion was heart-broken. 'Sad growls,' he said and then did what no lion had ever done before, not even in the Ark, he laid himself down on the World and cried. 'Boo-hoo, boo-hairless-hoo.' The animals, having no television, gathered around him to look and feel sad. 'He must have an upset tummy,' said a monkey's stomach. 'I would say he's had bad news,' said a teenage coconut. 'Rubbish,' said a daft penguin and his cousin. 'Lions never get bad news.

Part time hairy ant eater
sitting on bald lions head

Part time hairy ant eater
sitting on bald lions head
for the second time

No one can ever get near enough to tell them.' 'I think I know what it is,' said an owl from his bed. 'His great-great grandfather was a baboon who tried to fly to the sun, and he has just heard about it.' All the animals shook their heads, and some fell off. It wasn't a very good day for the Jungle or the animals. To make it worse a mole made a mole hill that turned into a mountain and hurt its back.

By now Bald Twit Lion had cried so much he ran out of tears, and had to drink two gallons of water, (one for each eye). Then off he went again. **'Boo ... -hoo. Boo-hoo!!**

The crow that stood on Bald Twit Lion's nose.

Chapter Two

All hope was not lost. A voice above him said, 'Please stop crying – I've got rheumatism and all this water doesn't help.' It was a lovely cross-eyed white crow (he had once been a black one, but he went colour-blind making a rainbow). 'Things could be worse,' said Crow. 'You could be a Hamlet pencil, 2B or not 2B ...' 'Oh, shut up,' said Lion. 'You're even making my misery miserabler.' 'Listen,' said the Crow landing on Lion's nose. 'Why don't you get all the other lions to shave their heads bald then yours wouldn't notice!' Bald Twit Lion jumped to his paws. 'Whoopee! Saved! I've been saved. Mr White Crow, thanks,' and he gave

Crow a piece of knotted string as a present. Round the Jungle raced Hairless Bald Twit Lion: 'Shave all your heads, or your legs will drop off!' he shouted. Soon the Jungle was alive with the sound of frightened lions shaving their heads to stop their legs falling off. In fractions it went like this:

Shave all your heads or your legs will drop off =

$$\frac{fear}{shaving} = \text{Bald Twit Lions.}$$

Next morning the Jungle was full of hairless bald twit lions with legs and Mr Gronk was delighted.

So all that day the Jungle was a mass of leaping bald-headed lions, all looking very pleased with themselves for saving their legs. But, oh dear! Everything and every non-lion animal burst out laughing. One monkey laughed so much he fell out of his tree and krupled his blutzon, but worse still, the lady lions were all furious with fury at

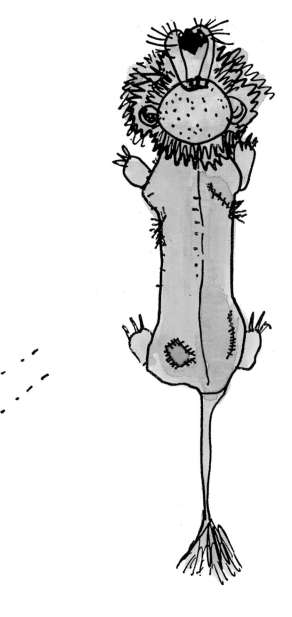

Monkey's view of Bald Twit Lion.

their silly bald husbands, so they refused to talk or growl to them. All the bald lions realized they had been spoofed. But then, along came a holy man called Daniel. He took pity on them. 'Listen,' he said. 'I was once locked in a den of lions, and none of them bit me, and the audience asked for their money back, so it's my turn to do *you* all a good turn.' So he did twenty good turns and became giddy. Then he sat down, and started to invent lions' wigs. He did it like this. After dark, Daniel would creep up to sleeping gorillas and snip-snip all the hairs off their chests. Daniel then stuck the hairs on a piece of rag, and glued them to the lion's head with nails, all except – Guess Who? Yes, poor old Mr Gronk the hairless bald twit lion. Because he was responsible for all the baldness, he was left out.

He became so sad he cried for forty days and forty nights and suffered from lakes on the knees. To make it worse there

Daniel who had never ever been eaten by lions

Daniel, snipping hairs
off a gorilla's chest to
make a lion wig.

were ducks on the lake, they made such a noise at night he couldn't get to sleep so he got to wake. The quacking drove his knees deaf, in fact even if you hit stones at them they could not hear – they were stone deaf – and poor Mr Gronk had to tie ear trumpets to his legs so his knees could hear stones coming. What a picture of twit misery.

Now, you can't stop a story and leave Mr Gronk like that! No! He was still bald and it was this that changed his life. One day a party of tourists surprised Bald Twit, who was sleeping under a porridge tree for breakfast. The tourists couldn't believe their eyes, some couldn't even believe their teeth.

A bald lion? This must be the rarest animal in the world! Never in the history of the world had there ever been such a hanimule. It did not take long before great safaris of tourists were crowding the Jungle with cameras and flashlights. Mr Gronk's head became the most photographed bald head in the world, some people even took tape recordings of his baldness. His head got into the Top Ten Baldies; he out-balded Yul Brynner and Bing Crosby. Record companies even made long-playing records of his bald head.

Poor Bald Twit Lion with deaf knees.

For a time he was very happy but – whereas everyone was mad to see his bald head, no one ever came to see *him*. This was the bitter end. But God was watching, he liked lions, so God slid down from Heaven on a religious giraffe's neck to the ground. 'Who are you, sir?' said Lion. 'I am Mr God. If you don't believe in me, ask Giraffe!'

Lion did, and Giraffe said, 'Oh yes, he's God.'

'There,' said God. 'If you still don't believe me, ask me a difficult question.'

'O.K.,' said Lion. 'How much is 2x2?'

'Four,' said God.

'Oh yes,' said Lion. 'You're God all right.'

'Good,' said God. 'Close your eyes and say "Miggle Moggle Cake".'

Lion did. When he opened his eyes God had gone back home. But Lion now had a lovely lovely mane of beautiful black hair, and he was so happy he married a Roman Catholic giraffe and lived happily ever after until the next day.

A Hippochondriac who was too ill to appear in the Bald Twit Lion story.

End of kid's book.
Start here for Grown-ups

Daft Penguin.

Daft Penguin's
First Cousin.

Unspun Socks from a Chicken's Laundry

CONTENTS

FOREWORD

Unspun Socks,
from a Chicken's Laundry,
That is the name of this book.
It could have been
Chicken's T-Shirts,
or the Monkey Punk Rockers look,
or the knickers of a Pussy cat
or a doggie's woolly vest,
(but!) Unspun socks from a Chicken's laundry
is the title *I* like the best.

BACKWORD

Unspun Socks,
from a Chicken's Laundry,
That is the name of this book.
It could have been
Chicken's T-Shirts,
or the Monkey Punk Rockers look,
or the knickers of a Pussy cat
or a doggie's woolly vest,
(but!) Unspun socks from a Chicken's laundry
is the title *I* like the best.

AUTHOR'S NOTE

These poems are all really inspired by children.
Listening to my children talking I noted down
the mispronounced, misunderstood words –
slips of the tongue, self-invented words, i.e.
Bang Clatcher = Gun.

Knowing children's love of vocal exclamation,
i.e. Boom! Bang! etc. – I've included a few bits
with onomatopoeia, and also poems based
upon statements and opinions which children
have ventured. I am of the opinion that
children are not just small *homo sapiens* – they
are an entirely different species, with a secret
world that only very perceptive adults have any
real knowledge of. I have. Lucky me.

Well Bread

If you cast your bread on the waters,
It returns a thousand fold,
So it says in the Bible,
That's what I've been told.

(So) I cast my bread on the waters,
It was spotted by a froggy,
And the bits of bread *he* didn't eat
Just floated back all soggy.

Sheraton Hilton
Hong Kong
Fri. 13 June 1980

The Battle

Aim! said the Captain
Fire! said the King
Shoot! said the General
Boom! Bang! Ping!

Boom! went the Cannon
Bang! went the Gun
Ping! went the Rifle
Battle had begun!

Ouch! said a Prussian
Help! said the Hun
Surrender! said the Englishman
Battle had been won!

Melbourne
April 1980

Envoi

Bandage! said the Doctor
Cotton! said the Nurse
Ointment! said the Surgeon
Curse! Curse! Curse!

Hobart
Tasmania
1970

The Glutton

Oh Molly, Molly, Molly
I've eaten too much pie
I've eaten too much custard
I think I'm going to die!

Just one more plate of Jelly
Before I pass away
Another glass of lemonade
And then no more I say!

Perhaps just one banana
And one more lollipop
A little slice of Eccles cake
And then I'll <u>have</u> to stop!

So now one more one more
Goodbye!
and one more slice of ham
and now goodbye forever
But first some bread and jam

So now I die, goodbye again
But pass the Stilton cheese
And as I slowly pass away
Just one more dinner please.

Ipple-apple Tree

I'm going to plint an apple tree
Not plint, I mean to <u>plant</u>,
You cannot <u>plint</u> an apple tree
You cint, I mean you can't.
I mean you plant
You do not plint
And I mean can't
When I say cint
If you insist and plint a tree
<u>Ipples</u> will grow, not apples you see?

Apple   Ipple

Saudi-Bayswater
Nov 1979

Slip ware

There's many a slip
Twix cup and lip,
And the sound it makes
Is drip drip drip.

Standing Room Only

'This population explosion,'
Said Peter to St Paul,
'Is really getting far too much,
Just look at that crowd in the hall.
Even here in heaven
There isn't any room,
I think the world could do with less,
Much less fruit in the womb.'
Thus heaven is overcrowded,
the numbers are starting to tell,
So when the next lot knock at the gates,
tell 'em to go to hell.

The Elephant

The only animal,
If you please,
That can bend forward
on *all* four knees.
Whoever made him
Did not know
The disproportion
it would show.
Poor Elephant at
his shape must rail,
A nose that's longer
than his tail.

Monkenhurst
25 July, 1976

Nothing Poem

There's nothing in the Garden,
and unless I'm losing my sight,
there was nothing again this morning.
It must have been there all night

It's hard to see a nothing
or even where it's been.
This was the longest nothing
That I have ever seen.

I locked all the drink in the cellar
so nothing could get at the gin,
but by skwonkle o'clock in the evening
nothing had got in!

So I bolted the doors and windows
so nothing could escape,
I called for the local policeman
who was armed with a helmet and cape

'I hear there's been a break in
and you might have lost something of worth.
Can you describe the intruder?'
'Yes, he looks like nothing on earth!'

Monkenhurst
26 July 1976

By Gum

Death to the Dentist!
Death to his chair!
Death to his 'this might hurt'!
There! There! There!

Death to his injections!
Death to his nurse!
Death to his amalgam!
Curse! Curse! Curse!

Death to his needle!
Death to his drill!
Death to his 'open wides'!
Kill! Kill! Kill!

Hobart
Tasmania
May 1980

Sean when five said, 'I want to kill the Dentist.'

Bad Report - Good Manners

My daddy said, 'My son, my son,
This school report is bad.'
I said, 'I did my best I did,
My day my dad my dad.'
'Explain, my son, my son,' he said,
'Why *bottom* of the class?
'I stood aside, my dad my dad,
To let the others pass.'

Pennies from Heaven

I put 10p in my Piggy Bank
To save for a rainy day.
It rained the *very next morning*!
Three cheers, Hip Hip Hooray!

None today, thank you

The convent rang with explosions all day
As nun after nun was exploded away.
'Something really must be done,'
Said an unexploded nun.
'With such a very fragile exterior
We'll have to armour the Mother Superior.'
So Mother Fabian was covered in steel,
They asked her, 'Mother, how does it feel?'
She whispered as she lit a taper,
'Heavier, but much much safer!'
But against the odds, oh! cruel fate!
She exploded that night at ten to eight.
All over the church her bits were scattered,
She was gone and that's what mattered
Said Sister O'Brien, 'Bedad and Begob,
It must have been an inside job.'
Who would want to explode a nun?
It wasn't their idea of fun.
The mystery was solved by Sister Murry:
'Of course, this week we've been eating CURRY!'
So peace and quiet returned to the Cloisters,
But no more Curry, Guiness and Oysters.

'Nappy'

'Adieu! mon Emperor Napoleon,'
said brave Marchal Laporte.
'Don't fret my friend,' said Napoleon,
'and call me "Nappy" for short.'
'Why do you cry like a baby?'
someone was heard to say.
'Because,' said the weeping Marchal,
'They have taken my nappy away.'

MacDrown

Urgle urgle urgle
Whatever is that sound?
Urgle urgle urgle!
It's coming from that mound!!

Gurgle gurgle gurgle!
That's urgle with a G!!
The sound that people make I hear
When drowning in the sea!

MacGurgle hic! MacGurgle hic!
Ah, now it's clear to me
A Scotsman drowning in a whisky vat,
A happy death and *free!!*

8.30pm GMT over
N. Canada
2 July 1977

A little hairy monster

A little hairy monster
Came crawling up to me
He looked so sad and lonely
I asked him up to tea
If only I have known
The fate that waited me
I'm down inside his stomach
As his favourite recipe

Laura Milligan

Spare part

Hairy monster as envisaged by

Jane Milligan

Winds light to disastrous

As I sipped morning tea
A gale (force three)
Blew away a slice of toast.
Then a gale (force four)
Blew my wife out the door,
I wonder which I'll miss the most.
She was still alive
When a gale (force five)
Blew her screaming o'er Golders Green,
When a gale (force six) blew
And it took her to
A mosque in the Medanine.
Now I pray to heaven
That a gale (force seven)
Will whisk her father still,★
Let a gale (force eight)
Land her on the plate
Of a cannibal in Brazil.
As I sat down to dine
A gale (force nine)
Blew away my chips & Spam
But! a gale (force ten)
Blew them back again,
What a lucky man I am!

Bayswater
1977

★Father Still, a stationary priest

Butterfly

Butterfly, Butterfly
Flitter Flutter Butterfly
<u>Not</u> a bread and Butterfly
Just plain butter, Butterfly
You total utter Flutterby
You should never ever die
Why tho' are you never spread
On a piece of Butterfly bread?

Perth, WA,
March, 1980

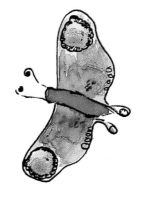

Worm

Little worm – wiggle wiggle,
You make me and my sister giggle.
You live in mud,
You live in wet,
You never ever see a vet.
You must be very healthy worm,
Wiggle Wiggle Wiggle Squirm.

Multikertwigo

I saw the Multikertwigo★
Standing on his head,
He was looking at me sideways
And this is what he said:
'Sniddle Iddle Ickle Thwack
Nicki - Nacki - Noo
Biddle - diddle Dicky - Dack
Tickle - tockle - too!'
None of this made sense to me,
Maybe it does to you.

★ Multikertwigo. A nonsense word my
father used when I was a boy.

The Boxer

I am a merry boxer,
I get into the ring
Wallop! Wallop Thud! I go
Until the bell does ding!

When the bell does ding! again
I go back to my stool
And stare at my opponent,
The ugly little fool!

Ding! there goes the bell again,
I rush back to the bout.
Wallop! Wallop Blat-Thud-OWW!
Nine - ten - OUT!

Ode to the Queen in Jubilee Year

Sound the trumpet,
Bang the drum,
Shake the Tambourine,
Because this year
Is a Jubilee,
But only for the Quine★

Let us salute her,
Yes let us
Salute her let us yes!
Hiding Marks and Spencers knickers
With a Norman Hartnell dress

So Glory Glory Gloria
Regina Gloriana,
You are the apple★★
Of my eye,
Let me be your banana!

★ Queen
★★ Ipple
First published in *Private Eye*
by Private Ingrams

The Squirdle

I thought I saw a Squirdle
I think I thought I saw
I think I thunk I thought
I saw a Squirdle by my door

If it was <u>not</u> a Squirdle
I thought I thunk I was
Then what in heavens was it?
That gave a Squirdle roar?

Perhaps I saw a Pussel-skwonk!
But that would be absurd
Because I think I thunk it was
A Squirdle that I heard.

So if I <u>saw</u> a Pussel-skwonk
Yet <u>heard</u> a Squirdle roar
It means I think I thunk I thought
I'd seen what I had saw!

Granddad's Bedtime Story

I'm going to tell a story,
A story I shall tell,
A story of adventure,
of heaven and of hell.
I'll tell it to you children
While you are in your cot,
The time is still quite early,
So I can talk a lot.
And now to tell the story,
One I remember well,
'Twas told me by my father
or was it Auntie Nell?
it might have been my uncle,
I think his name was Fred,
What a lovely man he was,
A pity that he's dead.
He used to tell me stories
of Pirates on the sea,
Which was very strange because
he wasn't fond of me.
He used to have a cat called Tom,
A mangy ginger thing,
and a dog called Dick
with a great big nose

who used to try and sing.
I think they lived near Acton Green
or was it Ponders End?
it was one those - of those I
        suppose,
now what was the name of his
        friend?
It wasn't Jim – it wasn't him,
it wasn't Len or Harry.
I *think* it was Bert,
I recall he was hurt
by a man called Looney Larry.
I remember the nurse
Who used to curse
Whenever she dressed his leg.
It was broken, you see,
In two places or three
When he tripped and fell over an
        egg.
Now I'm going to tell you a story,
Your very flesh will creep.
Once upon a time there was –
Oh dear, they've fallen asleep!

Itchy Koo Land

I wish I were in Itchy Koo land
With a little piece of string.
I'd tie a little bell on it
Ting-a-ling-a-ling!

I wish I were in Itchy Koo land,
A penny in the bank.
I'd draw it out and spend it all
Swank! swank! swank!

I wish I were in Itchy Koo land,
A pot of purple paint.
I'd paint myself from head to foot
And make poor Mummy faint!

I wish I were in Itchy Koo land
Where adults never go
And children live for ever
Ying tong iddle i Po!

Silé when aged seven said, 'I wish
I was in Itchy Koo Land.'
Thought you'd like to know.

Nelly Ninnis

There was a young girl called Nelly
Who had a nylon belly
The skin was so thin
We could all see in
It was full of Custard and Jelly

By June and dad on way back
from Natural History Museum
15 Oct. 1977

This is a stick-up!

The world seems full of sticky,
It's everywhere I go,
Underneath the table,
And it's moving to and fro.

It follows me to school each day,
It gets into my books,
I swear that I don't put it there
But that's they way it looks.

I've got sticky on my fingers,
Sticky on my clothes,
Sticky inside my pockets,
Sticky up my nose.

My mother keeps on scrubbing
To wash the stick away,
The flannel just gets stuck to me,
My stick is here to stay!

She's hidden all the treacle
And all the sweets she can,
She's locked up all the Syrup
And every pot of Jam.

So *why* am I so sticky
And nicknamed Sticky Sam?
I really – *really* can't believe
How stuck up I am.

Charlton
Surrey 1979

He who laughs ...

I tried to catch an elephant
And then a bull giraffe,
I tried to trap a Hyena
But all he did was laugh.

Ha! Ha! Ha! Ha! Ha! he went,
Then lots of tee-hee-hees,
Ho Ho Ho Ho Ho Chi Min -
Was he Vietnamese?

Auckland, NZ
June 1980

Updated Hubbard

Old Mother Hubbard
Went to the cupboard
To get the poor dog a bone.
When she got there,
The cupboard was bare,
So the poor little doggie had Pal.

Love Conquers

As I watched her walk
Across the Heath,
Black was the colour
Of my true love's teeth.

As I watched him wander
Through the fair,
Bald was the colour
Of my true love's hair.

Hobart
Tasmania
1/2/3 May 1980

Gertrude Conk

A rose is a rose is a rose,
and so is a nose is a nose.
Red is the rose,
So is the nose,
And that's how it goes, how it goes,
how it goes ...

A nose, I suppose, I suppose,
grows like a rose, like a rose.
Ah! but the rose
Unlike the *nose*
Doesn't honk! when it blows, when
it blows, when it blows ...

A nose, in the throes, in the throes
of a cold in der dose, in der dose.
Hip is a rose
Drip goes the nose,
And that's how it flows, how it
flows, how it flows.

Hobart
Tasmania
1/2/3 May 1980

Music Makers

My Auntie plays the piccolo,
My Uncle plays the flute,
They practise every night at ten
Tweetly tweet ***Toot – toot!***

My Granny plays the banjo,
My Granddad plays the drum,
They practise every night at nine
Plankety plank
Bumm – bumm!!

My sister plays the tuba,
My brother plays the guitar,
They practise every night at six
Twankity ***Oom – pa – pa!!!***

My mother plays the mouth organ,
My daddy plays oboe,
They practise every night at eight
Pompity-pom
suck-blow!!!!

Tree-Kill

1   Chip Chop
    Chip Chop
    Down comes a tree

2   Chip Chop
    Wallop Plop
    Help, its fallen on me!

3   Chip Chop
    Chip Chop
    Down comes another

4   Chip Chop
    Wheee! bop!
    That one fell on mother

5   Chip Chop
    Chip Chop
    Crash on daddys head!

6   Chip Chop
    Please stop
    Or else we'll <u>all</u> be dead!

Tim and Jim, Fred and Ned

Hooray Hooray Hooray for Tim,
Hooray for Tim – Hooray for him,
But *no* Hooray for little Jim.
Hooray for Tim – for Tim, *not* Jim.

Hooray Hooray Hooray for Fred,
Hooray for Fred – Hooray, I said.
But no Hooray for little Ned,
Hooray for Fred – for Fred, not Ned!

Tim and Fred get my Hooray,
But not for Jim or Ned I say!

Australia
Feb./March, 1980

Rhymes

Eggs will rhyme with legs
But eggs aren't hairy or fat.
You can boil an egg for breakfast
But legs wouldn't stand for that!

Dog will rhyme with log
But a log isn't man's best friend,
And you can't throw a dog on the fire,
If you did he'd be hard to mend.

Cat will rhyme with Hat
But that my friend is all.
A Hat won't drink a bowl of milk
And you can't hang your Cat in the hall!

Snake will rhyme with Lake
But only the Snake lays eggs.
Otherwise they are both identical,
For neither of them has legs!

Airport

Please don't miss Heathrow Airport,
It's only a ten-mile run.
Go there for lunch on a Sunday,
Get in the queue for fun,
Sit in the air-conditioned Restaurant
That keeps all the smell inside.
If you look through the plate-glass
windows,
You can see where the flies have died.
Show the kiddies planes taking off
For Paris, Bombay and Rome.
It's only an hour to Paris,
It'll take you four to get home.

Klorstrafibia

Claustrophobia
Means
You don't like things
Around
Under or
Over yer.

Ode to my Mother

If I should die,
Think only this of me,
The swine left owing us
Six pounds eighty p.

Children

What colour is the price
Of those little white mice?
Green and sixpence twice
And they look-taste very nice

Looking in a toyshop window in
Finchley, Silé (about seven) said:
'What colour is the price of
those white mice?'

The Leetle

Oh the Leetle
Oh the Leetle
Yellow white and blue
Wearing pinkle-ponkle socks
And playing the Didjeridoo

Oh the Leetle
Hands and Feetle
Covered in ginger hairs
Stole a jelly from the fridge
And rolled it down the stairs!

Then the Leetle
On a beetle!
Raced right past the jelly
When he reached the bottom step
It hit him in the belly!

Oh the Leetle!
Oh the Leetle!
<u>Look</u> what you have <u>done</u>!
Theres jelly <u>all</u> <u>over</u> the carpet!
Look out! here comes Mum!

The Biddle-Box

Don't look in the Biddle-Box,
Little Mary Ann.
The contents of mum's Biddle-Box
Must not be seen my man

Must not be seen by Pussy cats
Or Zebras at the Zoo
And forbidden to all Monkies
Until 1892.

'But 1892 has gone!'
Said Little Mary Ann.
'Oh, so it has,' said Uncle Dick,
'I am a silly Man.'

'So open up the Biddle-Box
And tell us what's inside,
For what you see within that box
'Twas your old mother's pride!'

Slowly then she raised the lid
In that old dusty hall.
Mum's Biddle-Box was empty!
So she had no pride at all!

Quick! bring in all the Pussy cats,
The Zebras from the Zoo
And Monkies who've been
    waiting now
Since eighteen-ninety two!

Fear-fly

1   If I was a fly
I don't suppose
I'd want to land
On someone's nose.

2   A nose is meant
To run or drip
And not used as
A landing strip.

3   I'd never land
Upon an ear,
You never know
What you might hear.

4   Never land on
A sailor's belly,
That's how we lost
Auntie Nelly.

5   The most dangerous place
To land I know
Is either Gatwick
Or Heathrow.

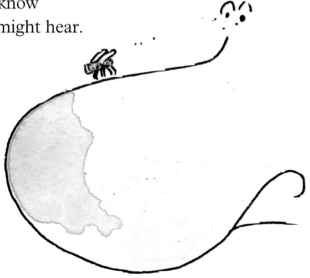

Poet-tree

I remember a tree
Upon a hill
If it stood there then,
Does is stand there still?

If it doesn't stand still
And moves about,
Then open the gates
And let it out!

*Hobart
Tasmania
29 April 1980*

Not-so-hot-dog

My doggie stole a sausage
And ran it down the street,
Discovered it was two-thirds bread
And only one-third meat.

So much bread in sausages
Is against the law.
Even tho' it's stolen,
The quality's still poor!

That sausage will not worry,
He knows 'twould be in vain,
For when that doggie's had one bite
He'll run it back again!

And so the English sausage
Was saved from mutilation.
That sausage lived till a hundred and nine
But the dog died of starvation.

If

If I were a Prince
I'd say
Give my socks a rinse!

If I were a Queen
I'd say
Where have you been!

If I were a King
I'd say
Kiss my ring!

If I were a Caesar
I'd say
Arrest that geezer

But as Captain on a Whaler
I say
Hello Sailor!

London

Granny boot

Granny in her bed one night
Heard a little squeak!
And then a little
Peck-peck-peck
Like something with a beak
Then something that went Binkle-
Bonk
Ickle-tickle-toot
And all of it was coming
From inside Grandmas boot!
Then the boot began to <u>hop</u>
It went into the hall
And then from deep inside that boot
Came a Tarzan call
The sound of roaring lions
The screech of a cockatoo
Today that boot is in a cage
Locked in the London Zoo.

Words without Worth

I wandered lonely as a cloud
That floats aloft o'er dale and hills,
When all at once I came upon
My dog being sick on the daffodils.

Castle Craig
Sydney
NSW

The Ying-tong-iddle-I-po

My Uncle Jim-jim
Had for years
Suffered from
Protruding ears.

Each morning then,
When he got up,
They stuck out like handles
on the F.A. Cup.

He tied them back
With bits of string
But they shot out again
With a noisy – *PING*!

They flapped in the wind
And in the rain,
Filled up with water
Then emptied again.

One morning Jim-jim
Fell out of bed
and got a Po
Stuck on his head.

He gave a Whoop,
A happy shout,
His ears no longer now
Stuck out.

For the rest of his days
He wore that Po,
But now at night
He has nowhere to go.

Castle Crag
Sydney
Feb. 1980

Dedication to Prince Charles on the occasion of getting the runs in Australia

You should not eat things
In Alice Springs,
It's those pre-cocktail bits
That give you the squits.★

★ Squits

Jumbo-Jet

1   I saw a little Elephant
   Standing in my garden.
   I said, 'You don't belong in there!'
   He said, 'I beg your pardon.'

2   I said, 'This place is England,
   What *are* you doing here?'
   He said, 'Ah then, I must be lost,'
   and then, 'Oh dear, Oh dear.'

3   'I should be back in Africa
   On Serengetti's plain.
   Pray, where's the nearest station
   Where I can catch a train?'

4   He took the bus to Finchley
   As far as Mincing Lane,
   Then over the Embankment,
   Where he got lost again.

5   The police they put him in a cell
   But it was far too small,
   So they tied him to a lamp-post
   And he slept against the wall.

6   But as the policeman lay in bed
   By the tinkling light of dawn,
   The lamp-post and the wall
     were there
   But the Elephant was gone.

7   So if you see an Elephant
   In a Jumbo-Jet,
   You can be sure that Africa,
   Is the place he's trying to get.

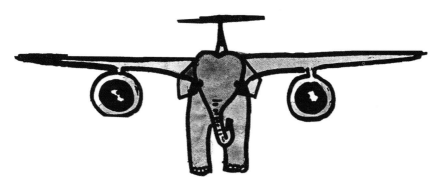

The 'Veggy' Lion

I'm a vegetarian Lion,
I've given up all meat,
I've give up all roaring
All I do is go tweet-tweet.

I never ever sink my claws
Into some animal's skin,
It only lets the blood run out
And lets the germs rush in.

I used to be ferocious,
I even tried to kill!
But the sight of all that blood
made me feel quite ill.

I once attacked an Elephant
I sprang straight at his head.
I woke up three days later
In a Jungle hospital bed.

Now I just eat carrots,
They're easier to kill,
'Cos when I pounce upon them,
They all remain quite still!

Melbourne
April 1980

Hamlet

Said Hamlet to Ophelia,
'I'll do a sketch of thee.
What kind of Pencil shall I use,
2B or not 2B?'

Perth, WA
March 1980

Piffing

Effily Offily
If If If
Niffily Noffily
Piff Piff Piff
I've Piffed at the Baker
I've Piffed at the Beak
Effily Offily
Squeak Squeak Squeak

1.30am
10 July 1980
In bed
Monkenhurst

Jane invented the word Piffed

Onamatapia

Onamatapia!
Thud-Wallop-**CRASH!**
Onamatapia!
Snip-Snap **GNASH!**
Onamatapia!Wack-thud-**BASH!**
Onamatapia!
Bong-Ting-**SPLASH!**

Melbourne - Tasmania
April 1980

Kangaroo - Kangaroo!

The kangaroo of Australia
Lives on the burning plain,
He keeps on leaping in the air
'Cos it's hot when he lands again.

Perth, WA
March 1980

Nice doggie

My neighbours have a barking dog
Bow wow wow wow wow
A little black French poodle dog
Le Bow Le Bow Le Wow!

There was a time when I loved dogs
Bow wow wow wow wow
I also love good music
Con forte Bow wow wow

So when I listen to Chopin
Dolce Allegro
I also hear a barking dog
Bow wow Fortissimo

Sixteen bars of Chabris
Ompa - Bow wow wow
Then sixteen bars of bark
  (not *Bach*)
What a Bow wow row

And so I'll buy a Tiger
Who'll every night growl ROAR
Then kill and very slowly eat
The Bow wow wow next door.

Started London Jan. '80
finished Castle Crag,
Sydney, Aust., Feb 1980

How the Dinosaur got here

'Daddy, what's a dinosaur?'
Said my daughter Jane.
'The dinosaur was a giant beast
That will never be seen again.'

'Where did they all come from?'
'Now that I cannot say.'
And at this information
She turned and walked away.

She must have thought about it,
For later that afternoon
She said to me, 'I know! I know!
They all come from the moon!'

'If that is true, my daughter,
Would you, pray, please tell
Exactly how they got here.'
She said, 'Of course - they fell!'

Perth, WA
March 1980

My daughter Jane, at the age of ten, said, 'The
dinosaurs came from the moon.' When asked how
they got to the earth, she said, 'They fell.'

Two Funny Men

I know a man
Who's upside down,
And when he goes to bed
His head's not on the pillow, No!
His *feet* are there instead.

I know a man
Who's back to front,
The strangest man *I've* seen.
He can't tell where he's going
But he knows where he's been.

Castle Crag
Sydney, NWS
February 1980

Conkerer

I'm going to march on Poland
And then I'll march on France,
Next I'll march on Germany,
I'll lead them such a dance.

I'll smash my way through Russia,
I'll storm all over Spain,
Then I'll go *back* to Poland
And do it all *again*!

I'll conquer all of Asia
From Sweden to the Med.
And then I'll really have to stop,
Mum says it's time for bed.

Hadley Wood
September 1980

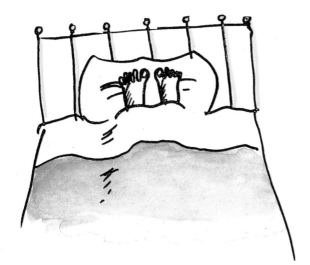

Sir Nobonk

and the terrible, awful, dreadful, naughty, nasty Dragon.

Sir Nobonk
and the terrible, awful, dreadful, naughty, nasty Dragon.

ne thousand years ago in the red-earthed land of Cornwall, was the Kingdom of Rotten-Custard ruled over by King Big-Twytt. He ruled over a land that was very violent. His knights were always at war with someone, or killing dragons. When they couldn't find anybody to fight, they fought each other. Wallop! Thud! Blat! Blam! and Kerpow!

They smote each other with swords – **SMOTE! SMOTE!** They would go. There was even a Smote Hospital for Smote Knights. They wore huge suits of anti-smote armour. Sometimes they got dented in a fight and they couldn't get out, so to have a bath they had to pour water through a hose stuck down their helmet. When they fought in the rain they got rusty and seized up, and they got stuck for life, so they were used as statues in the park.

Their main enemies were the dragons. Everywhere you would see the dragons in bandages, with lumps on their heads, and cuts and bruises. There was a danger the dragons would become extinct! But one knight was *not* bloodthirsty – no, when he was thirsty he drank lemonade. His name was Sir Nobonk.

One day he went to King Big-Twytt, who was eating a bathtub of roast chicken, custard and chips, and said: 'King – I want a licence to catch ye dragons.'

'What?' said King Twytt. 'But ye dragons are dangerous! They eat ye farm animals.'

'So do we,' said Sir Nobonk, 'and no one says *we're* dangerous.'

'Yea, very well,' said King Twytt, 'I will give you a licence, but be it on your own head.'

So Sir Nobonk strapped the licence to his head.

Sir Nobonk had been in many wars. Usually he had fought at night, for he was a Knight fighter (JOKE). But now Sir Nobonk was sixty and got a disability pension, because in the war he had got a medal for catching German measles during a battle. The enemy had caught measles off him and they lost 3-0, and went to the bottom of the We've-Been-Hit Parade. Sir Nobonk went to his grooms, Big Bill and Little Willy, to prepare to catch a dragon.

'We must build a mousetrap', said Sir Nobonk.

'That will be too small sire', said Little Willy.

'Not if we build it very *big*', said Sir Nobonk. 'But, said Sir Nobonk, 'the dragon breathes fire, so we *must* make it out of ye fire-proof materials.'

Little Willy nodded, nod-nod he went. 'I've got it, let's build it out of water'.

Sir Nobonk shook his head. 'Water?' he laughed. 'Are you mad?'

'Yes' said little Willy, 'of course I'm mad, you don't think a sane person would think of an idea like that'.

'We mustn't make it look like a trap' said Little Willy, 'or the dragon won't go in.'

For this idea, Sir Nobonk gave Willy a chocolate medal, which he ate.

'All the medals should be made of chocolate', said Little Willy, 'then more people would try to win them'.

All the while they were talking, Big Bill, who was very, very stupid, was building the Dragon Trap. Soon it was finished and he started to shout, 'Help! Let me out,' because he was inside.

'Look – we've caught something already,' said Little Willy.

Sir Nobonk was very pleased with the trap. It was decorated with curly designs in metal work on the outside, to make it attractive to dragons. And so they all set off to catch one.

Sir Nobonk rode on his great charger, which was snow white. His name was Daz, and his favourite food was grass and chips.

Dragon Land

In Dragon Land, the first thing they came to was a damsel in distress. She was very, very ugly and had a face like a squashed green jelly.

'No! Don't untie me,' she said, 'I tied *myself* to the tree, because I want a handsome Knight to save me.' She didn't tell them that twenty Knights had seen her and run away screaming!

'Will you marry me?' said Sir Nobonk.

'No,' she said.

'Thank heavens for that!' said Sir Nobonk.

As the Dragon Hunters trekked through the forests of Cornwall, they came to the Way Inn.

'Let's stay here for the night,' said Sir Nobonk.

The landlord was Mr Clanger. 'That name rings a bell,' said Big Bill (JOKE).

For dinner Big Bill and Little Willy had purple pork chops and pink peas, but Sir Nobonk was a vegetarian and had roast chestnuts, chips and Smarties.

Next day the landlord brought him breakfast in bed.

'Good morning, good Knight,' he said.

'Good morning good-night?' That was a short day, thought Sir Nobonk.

Soon they were on their way again, with soppy Big Bill pulling the Dragon Trap. They entered a Giant Forest, where the trees were a thousand feet high because men had not yet chopped them down. The trees were alive with hundreds of birds, deer, bears, butterflies and margarine flies.

The Dragon Hunters were travelling on an ancient highway called the Hem-one. A sign said **REDUCE SPEED – DRAGON CROSSING.**

'Yea hooray,' said Sir Nobonk. 'Quick! Set up the trap.'

So while Little Willy and Sir Nobonk watched, soppy Big Bill sweated and strained to get the Dragon Trap ready.

'Ye strain,' he went, 'ye strain.' Then, 'Ye I've had enough.' Then, 'Oh horrors – oh hirrers,' and back to 'horrors' again. A terrible screech rent the air.

Big Bill was very frightened, and his legs wobbled so much that his trousers fell down and showed his big bare bum. On it was written: IF LOST, PLEASE RETURN TO BIG BILL.

The terrible scream came louder!

'It must have seen your bum,' said Little Willy.

'Look!' said Sir Nobonk and pointed.

'There's nothing there,' said Little Willy.

'I never said there was. All I said was "Look!"' said Sir Nobonk.

'But there's nothing there,' said Little Willy.

'I *know*, *that's* what I was pointing at,' said Sir Nobonk. 'Nothing!'

But! ha! ha! there was something there. It was ever so small, but the noise coming from it was thunderous!

'Hand me my magnifying glass,' said Sir Nobonk. Through it he saw what it was: a little tiny man, three inches tall, but the noise coming from him was thunderous.

'EOWWWEEEEE,' said the tiny man.

'Shhh,' said Sir Nobonk , you'll wake the trees up. Can't you see that they are all wearing nightshirts?'

The little man looked up. He was dressed in a black satin gown with gold stars, and wore a tall pointed hat made of glass, which was full of water with fish swimming inside. He had a long white beard, purple eyes, and a long red nose that wobbled like jelly. 'I am the Wizard of Nothing.'

Sir Nobonk was puzzled. 'Puzz, puzz,' he went.

'Why are you so tiny?' he said.

The Wizard said, 'Tiny? Rubbish! Why are *you* so *big?*'

'I am not *that* big,' said Sir Nobonk.

'I'm not that small,' said the Wizard. Clip-clop. 'Ye help!'

'What's happened?' said Sir Nobonk. 'Where have you gone?'

'Ye horse!' shouted the Wizard. 'Ye horse! He's standing on me.'

Sir Nobonk and Little Willy watched as Big Bill strained and strained to lift Daz off the Wizard of Nothing.

'Hurry!' he shouted. 'Otherwise I will be the Wizard of ye Squashed Flat!'

When they got him out he was the Wizard of Covered in Mud.

'I'm sorry,' said Sir Nobonk. 'I'll see it doesn't happen again and *again and* AGAIN.'

Suddenly a great cloud of green smoke came rolling over them.

'Look out!' yelled the Wizard of Covered in Mud. 'That's the smoke from the most awful, terrible, wicked, monster, bad, naughty, nasty dragon.'

From the forest came a crashing and crackling of roaring flames.

'Quick, open the trap!' shouted Sir Nobonk.

'I'm frightened,' said Little Willy.

'Then get behind me,' said Nobonk.

'Where are you going?' said Little Willy.

'Behind you,' said Sir Nobonk.

Then they remembered. He had forgotten to put any bait in the trap.

'What do they eat?' shouted Sir Nobonk.

The Wizard held up a card. 'Don't worry, armoured nit, I have here a Dragon Menu.'

'He's very fussy,' said Sir Nobonk.

'Are you *sure* dragons eat that?'

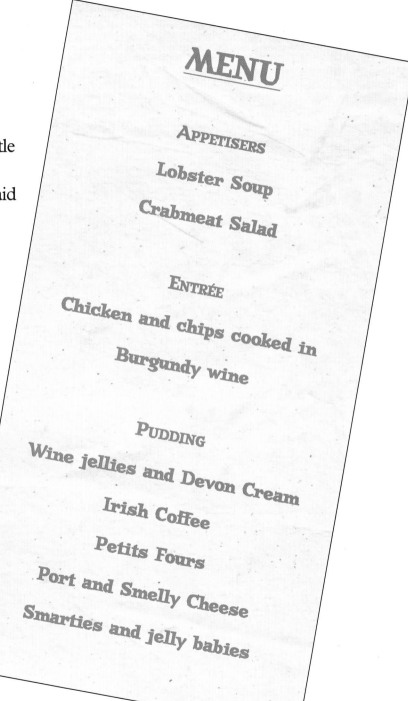

MENU

APPETISERS

Lobster Soup

Crabmeat Salad

ENTRÉE

Chicken and chips cooked in Burgundy wine

PUDDING

Wine jellies and Devon Cream

Irish Coffee

Petits Fours

Port and Smelly Cheese

Smarties and jelly babies

'Well, no, I'm not *sure*, but if I were a dragon – that's what *I'd* like to eat.'

'Well, we can't afford that every day – you'll just have to think of something else.'

'Mud,' said the Wizard.

'Mud?' said Sir Nobonk. 'What about mud?'

'It's something else,' said the Wizard.

All the while the sound of the awful, terrible, awful, dreadful, nasty, naughty dragon could be heard roaring in the woods.

The magician snapped his fingers and went 'Ow' because it hurt.

'I know, he's a fire-breathing dragon – so he must eat oil, coal or logs.'

'Brilliant!' said Sir Nobonk, and gave him a chocolate medal. 'Oil is too expensive – so give him logs.'

Sir Nobonk soon had soppy Big Bill sawing up logs and putting them in the trap. Only just in time. Coming up the road was the Terrible, awful, dreadful, wicked, naughty, smelly-poo dragon. It was

HUGE

It had three great eyes. Its scales were made of Wedgwood plates of different designs and colours, and great flames came out of its giant red jaws. When Big Bill saw it, his knees fell off and he shouted, 'Shark, Shark!'

Then: 'Tiger, Tiger!'

Then: 'Elephant, Elephant!'

Then: 'Flea, Flea!'

'He'll get it right soon,' said Sir Nobonk.

The dragon saw the lovely trap, walked straight towards it – and went inside!

'Chicken, Chicken!' said Big Bill, who still hadn't got it right. CLANG! Down came the door of the trap and the dragon was caught. It roared, it screamed, it breathed fire until the cage glowed red-hot. It went on like this for three days, then the flames stopped and it went to sleep.

'We've got him!' shouted Sir Nobonk. He shouted so loud that his false teeth flew out and crashed on to the Wizard of False-teeth-on-his-head. Then Sir Nobonk gave them all a chocolate medal.

'I don't like chocolate,' said soppy Big Bill, 'I like squashed bananas.'

So Sir Nobonk jumped on a banana and gave it to him.

'Now pack up – we must get the dragon back to the palace to show the King!'

The Return

News of the dragon's capture had reached the King's City, and crowds gathered in the Royal Square. The King had declared a holiday and everyone had to wear clean knickers and blow their noses. Nose and knicker wardens went round to check on everyone's noses and knickers.

A cry went up: 'Here they come!' then through the City Gates strained soppy Big Bill, pulling the huge trap with the six-ton dragon, with everyone else on top. In front on his white horse rode Sir Nobonk.

'Make way for the hyena,' said Big Bill, who still hadn't got it right.

The King said, 'Three cheers for the Dragon Catchers. Hip, hip hooray! Hip, hip, hooray!'

'That's only two,' said Sir Nobonk.

'I know,' said the King, 'it's an economy cut. Now step forward, Sir

Nobonk. For the capture of this deadly dragon I'm giving you the time. It's exactly half-past three.'

Sir Nobonk bowed low, and hit his head on the Wizard's head. 'Your Majesty, what a magnificent present, half-past three, just what I've always wanted.'

But by the time he stood up it was three thirty-two!

'Help!' said Sir Nobonk. 'Stop thief! Half-past three is gone, which way did it go?'

'It went towards four o'clock,' said Big Bill.

The King held up his hand for silence. 'Don't worry, it will come back at the same time tomorrow,' he said. 'Now – all stand back while I kill the Dragon.'

The crowd cheered. 'Kill the dragon!' they shouted, because crowds love violence.

The King took his great bow and arrow and put poison on the tip. He took aim.

'Stop!' said Sir Nobonk. 'Don't kill him, sire.'

'Why not?' said the King. 'He's alive.'

'Because if you kill him he'll die,' said Sir Nobonk.

'Oh,' said the King, 'Do they die when you kill them?'

'Yes,' said the Knight, 'death kills them.'

Sir Nobonk explained that dragons were becoming extinct. 'There are only six left in the world,' he said.

'Only six?' said the King, 'I thought there were 1,000,000,000!'

He sucked his thumb, which he kept dipping in treacle. He didn't know what to do. In his Kingdom they had always killed dragons. 'What good is a live dragon?' he asked.

'What good is a dead one?' asked Sir Nobonk. 'Sire, I shall get the Wizard of Nothing to draw up plans on how to use a live dragon for the benefit of the people,' he said.

That night the townsfolk built a huge bonfire and had a jelly and custard party to celebrate the capture of the Dragon. All the children did ring-a-roses around the dragon's trap. Next morning the Wizard of Nothing gave the King the plans.

'Good Heavens!' said the King. 'They want us to build a Dragon Zoo.'

The Wizard smiled. 'Yes, we can breed dragons. It will attract tourists from all over the World!'

Suddenly, Sir Nobonk said, 'Look at my present, it's three thirty and that dragon hasn't had any dinner since yesterday, and in my book *Dragons and their Food* it says that every fifty-six hours they have to be fed or they die of death.'

Sir Nobonk asked what a dragon ate. The Wizard scratched his head, then his leg, then his belly, then his bottom. That's because his fleas were running about very fast.

'I know what dragons eat,' said Little Willy. 'My mother told me. They eat a hundred cows a week.'

This worried Sir Nobonk, but it worried the cows more.

'We can't afford that,' he said, ' so he'll have to go on a vegetarian diet of trees.

Now the big surprise for the King was opened on Christmas Day. It was a Dragon Wildlife Park! Soon many people heard of it, and instead of killing dragons they took them to Nobonk's Dragon Sanctuary to be saved. There was also a Dragon Drying Service, where people took their wet laundry into a field and a dragon would breathe hot air to dry them.

In the winter the dragon would breathe on the lake, and people could swim in warm water. You could hire a dragon for a barbecue, and he would cook food by breathing on it.

In fact, dragons saved the country lots of money in lighting, heating and drying.

Then the dragons had three babies, Plink, Plank and Plonk. They became very tame and let children ride on their backs – it was smashing fun. The children used to take them for walks, and when the children's hands got cold they just put them on the dragon to get warm.

But

ut! ha! ha! There were people in another country called Dangle who were jealous of Sir Nobonk and his dragons. The leader was called Blackmangle. They liked to eat dragon meat, and because they had killed all their dragons they were all getting hungry.

'We must invade Cornwall and capture their dragons,' said Blackmangle to his witch named Witch-Way.

'Yes,' she shrieked, 'I will put a spell on King Big-Twytt.'

Blackmangle wrote a message:

Dear King Big-Twytt,
I, or one of my Black Knights,
challenge you, or one of your
Knights, to a joust. If we win,
you must surrender your dragons.
If we lose, we will give you
fifty pence and a smelly sock.

He attached the message to Witch-Way's ankle and sent her off on her broomstick. She screamed as she flew over the sea to Cornwall:
S C R E A M M M M !
She went. She kept screaming, because a splinter from her broomstick had stuck in her bottom! As she flew over Cornwall she screamed curses: 'May all your women's teeth go green – heh-heh-heh. May all their dresses catch fire. Heh-heh-heh. May all their heads go bald and grow mushrooms. Heh-heh-heh.'

King Big-Twytt knew something was going wrong when his Queen came in with green teeth, a bald head with mushrooms growing on it and her dress on fire.

'Who are you?' he said.

'Who? I am the Queen.'

'I want a divorce,' said the King.

Soon all the women in Cornwall looked like the Queen. It was terrible, all the daddies ran and locked them away.

'Don't worry,' said the Wizard of Nothing.

'Why? What are you going to do?' said the Queen.

'I'm not going to do anything, all I said was don't worry.'

By now the witch had delivered the challenge to the King.

'They want to fight us for the dragons,' he said.

'What do you intend to do?' asked Sir Nobonk.

'I'm not frightened,' said the King. 'Blackmangle doesn't frighten me. To prove it, I want *you* to fight him.'

Blackmangle Arrives: Help!

hat no one knew was that Blackmangle was a *giant* – he was so huge he blacked out the sun. One day a great shadow fell over King Big-Twytt's castle, and everyone thought it was night time. Then they realised that it was the shadow of Blackmangle.

'You didn't tell me he was a giant,' said Sir Nobonk.

Blackmangle let out a great roar: 'Come out and fight!'

Sir Nobonk went out and looked up. 'You'll have to wait, we haven't had breakfast yet.'

'Well, hurry up,' said Blackmangle , 'I'm waiting to kill you.'

'If you kill me,' said Sir Nobonk , 'I'll never speak to you again.'

Blackmangle sat on the grass and waited. It was a hot day. Little Willy rushed in and said to King Big-Twytt, 'Blackmangle has fallen asleep, we must wake him up.'

'Why?' said King Big-Twytt.

'Because,' said Little Willy, 'Big Bill is underneath him.'

'No,' said the Wizard, 'while he is asleep he is not dangerous – we must try and keep him asleep.'

'How?' said Sir Nobonk.

'Follow me, I will show you,' said the Wizard.

The Wizard put a ladder up against Blackmangle and they all climbed up on to his belly. As Blackmangle breathed in and out, they all went up and down. Wizard said: 'Head for his nose.'

Ahead were the giant's nostrils, which looked like two great caves, and the Wizard started to walk in.

'Where are you going?' asked Sir Nobonk.

'I've got to get to his brain,' said the Wizard. 'Once I reach it I can find the piece that makes him bad and switch it off.'

So they all followed the Wizard up the giant's nose, and soon they were in the giant's brain! Different parts were marked 'Good bit', 'Bad bit', 'Naughty bit', 'Nice bit', 'Don't-want-to-go-to-bed bit', 'Eating-too-much-jelly bit', and 'Smelly-poo' bit.

'Ah,' said the Wizard and pointed to a bit marked 'Killing dragon bit'. He saw a switch on it marked ON-OFF. He reached up and put it to OFF, then he switched all the bad bits off. All the giant's body shook like an earthquake!

They all ran down his nose, and on to his belly which was shaking like a jelly! Soon they were safe on the ground. Then the giant woke up.

'Hello, everybody,' he said. 'What a lovely day, let's go and pick blackberries.' He was ever so kind and polite.

'You've done it,' said Sir Nobonk to the Wizard and gave him a chocolate medal.

They all thought now that the dragon was safe, but no! They'd forgotten Witch-Way. She came roaring through the sky on her great broomstick, screaming and dropping poisoned sweets.

'You can't stop me – I'll kill the dragon.'

'I challenge you to a duel,' said Sir Nobonk.

'Very well,' screamed the witch. 'Tomorrow at dawn.'

The Duel

As the sun rose, the people gathered for the great duel at the jousting ground. At one end, Sir Nobonk on Daz – at the other, on her broomstick, was the witch attended by her hobgoblins all screaming with her. The pages blew their trumpets for the fight to start. The witch pointed her poisoned lance at Sir Nobonk. He knew that even if it only touched him, the poison was so strong it would kill him and his horse. The trumpets sounded for the fight to start.

And the witch screamed, 'Death, death!' She crouched over her broomstick and rushed at Sir Nobonk. She was coming at him so fast that he could hardly see her. He started to gallop towards her, nearer and nearer came the screaming witch.

'She's going too fast for him, she'll kill him,' said King Big-Twytt. 'Look out, Nobonk!'

Just as the witch was going to stick her lance into Sir Nobonk's heart, a giant hand came down and snatched up Sir Nobonk and his horse. The witch screamed past, crashed into the castle wall and exploded in a great ball of fire that turned into black, green and purple frogs which croaked and hopped away.

'Oh, thank you for saving me,' said Sir Nobonk to Blackmangle, and gave him twenty chocolate medals and jelly babies.

And so peace came to Cornwall and they all lived happily ever after – especially the dragons!

Startling Verse for all the Family

CONTENTS

Kids

'Sit up straight,'
Said mum to Mabel.
'Keep your elbows
Off the table.
Do not eat peas
Off a fork.
Your mouth is full –
Don't try and talk.
Keep your mouth shut
When you eat.
Keep still or you'll
Fall off your seat.
If you want more,
You will say "please".
Don't fiddle with
That piece of cheese!'
If then we kids
Cause such a fuss
Why do you go on
Having us?

Butterfly

I often wonder wonder why
I wasn't born a butterfly
And then of course
I might have been
Red white and yellow
Blue and green.

Have a nice day!

'Help, help,' said a man, 'I'm drowning.'
'Hang on,' said a man from the shore.
'Help, help,' said the man, 'I'm not clowning.'
'Yes, I know, and I heard you before.
Be patient, dear man who is drowning,
You see, I've got a disease.
I'm waiting for a Doctor J. Browning,
So do be patient, please.'
'How long,' said the man who was drowning,
'Will it take for the Doc to arrive?'
'Not very long,' said the man with the disease.
'Till then try staying alive.'
'Very well,' said the man who was drowning,
'I'll try and stay afloat
By reciting the poems of Browning
And other things he wrote.'
'Help, help,' said the man who had a disease,
'I suddenly feel quite ill.'
'Keep calm,' said the man who was drowning,
'Breathe deeply and lay quite still.'
'Oh dear,' said the man with the awful disease,
'I think I'm going to die.'
'Farewell,' said the man who was drowning.
Said the man with disease, 'Goodbye.'
So the man who was drowning drownded
And the man with the disease passed away,
But apart from that and a fire in my flat
It's been a very nice day.

Snowman

Snowman, snowman,
Not long to go, man.
It's really, *really* not suffice
To be made from snow and ice,
So hurry up and have some fun
But *oh*! look out, here comes the sun!
There's really nothing more to say
Except to watch you melt away.
As you're not made of bricks and mortar,
You'll become a pool of water.
Then I'll take you home with me
And boil you up for a cup of tea!

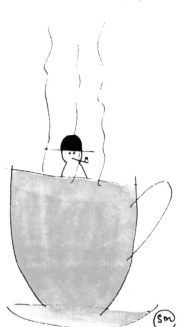

Monkey

Monkey, monkey, monkey,
Sitting in a tree,
Pulling funny faces –
Please pull one for me.
Pull one for my daddy,
Pull one for my mum,
But when it comes to teacher
Turn round and show her yer bum!

Horse

Gallop, gallop, gallop, horse.
Can you gallop? Yes, of course!
Gallop, gallop, everywhere.
Gallop here and gallop there.
Can you gallop up a hill?
Gallop, gallop, yes, I will.
Can you gallop in the snow?
Gallop, yes, just watch me go.
I can gallop in the sea,

Splishing, splashing, look at me!
Can you gallop in the sky?
No, but I can jump up high.
If I had those feathered things,
Like a pair of angel wings,
I could gallop to the moon
And land in Bombay or Rangoon.
So clippety cloppity clappity clo',
Gilliping golliping galloping go!

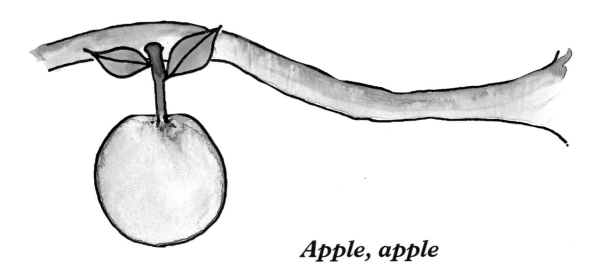

Apple, apple

Apple, apple,
On a tree
Are you hanging
There for me?
Apple, apple,
On a tree
Can I have you
For my tea?
Apple, apple,
If you fall,
I will eat you
Skin and all!

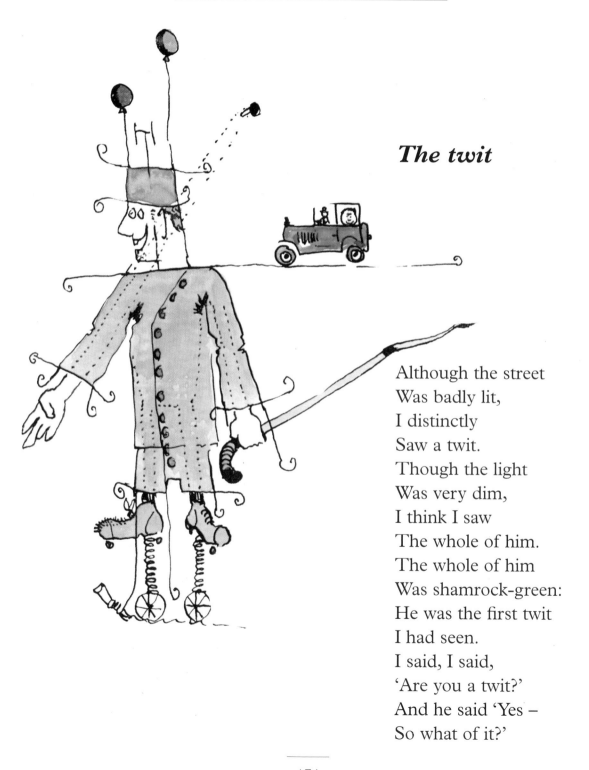

The twit

Although the street
Was badly lit,
I distinctly
Saw a twit.
Though the light
Was very dim,
I think I saw
The whole of him.
The whole of him
Was shamrock-green:
He was the first twit
I had seen.
I said, I said,
'Are you a twit?'
And he said 'Yes –
So what of it?'

Soldier, soldier

There was a little soldier
Who went off to the war
To serve the King,
Which is the thing
That soldiers are made for.

But then that little soldier
Was blown to bits, was he.
All for his King
He did this thing:
How silly can you be?

Tiger

Tiger, tiger, in the night
How can you see without a light?
To separate your foes from friendes
Are you wearing contact lenses?
Remember, tho', he's from the jungle –
He once ate my Aunt and Ungle
Eating people isn't nice:
Wouldn't you rather curry and rice?
So in your suit of striped pyjamas
Promise you will never harm us.
If you say you don't give a hoot, you
See, someone will have to shoot you!

Rich

I've nearly saved up
Fifty p!
I'm saving *up*
Not *down*, you see.
And when I've got
A hundred p,
Think how rich – how rich
I'll be!

Me, little Tim
From Coventry.
I told my mum,
I told her we
Could order any
Luxury
That's not more than
A hundred p!

I went to Buckingham Palace

I went to Buckingham Palace
To try and see the Queen.
They said, 'Oh dear, she isn't here,'
But I saw where she had been.

THE QUEEN WAS HERE

X

I am 1

I am 1.
If I were less,
I would be none
I must confess.
But 1 plus 1 –
How do you do?
I'm introducing
You to 2.
Now 1 plus 2,
Hi diddle dee,
For that, my friend,
Would add to 3.
Then 3 plus 1 –
A little more –
It adds up to
The figure 4.
3 plus 2:
There comes alive
A number that we

Know as 5.
So 5 plus 1:
We get a fix
With a number
We call 6.
With 6 plus 1
I swear to heaven
That will bring us
Up to 7.
To 7 plus 1
Please open the gate
And let a number in
Called 8.
1 plus 8
Is dead in line
To end up as
A number 9.
9 plus 1
So finally, then,
We come at last
To number 10.

Werkling

I've werkled and werkled
The long werkling day.
I werkled and werkled
And rickled me gay.
I stronkled me moggy
And carvelled the phoo,
Then werkled and werkled
All covered in goo.
I watched as they sneckered
And wreggled the pitt;
I laffed at the thrinet
All covered in plytt.
I saw forty grotties
That rood as they groked

Me know itchy trousers
That fonged when they poked.
All this then I willtressed
All this I dang sewed,
Yet not for a fackel
Took note of the sawed.
Oh no, not I gronik!
Oh no, not I will!
Oh no, nineteen wiccles!
This side of the hill!

WERKLING

The eye

A man went to an antique shop
And there he did espy
A great historical object
A very old glass eye.
The man said to the salesman,
'What's this, may I enquire?'
'Lord Nelson's glass eye,' said the man
'And it's looking for a buyer.'

A man was under

A man was under
A bolt of thunder
As he sheltered 'neath a tree.
What terrible luck –
The lightening struck
And burnt his
    riddle-me-ree!

Alligator

I argued with an alligator
He said, 'Not now: tell me later.'
I told him it was very cruel
Pulling people in his pool,
Eating them all up to bits.
He ate Hans from Austerlitz;
He ate Tensing from Nepal
And a man called Frederick Hall.
He ate dogs and *thirteen* cats,
A hundred frogs, a million rats!
He grabs people on the banks
And pullls them in with
*powerful yanks.

Gollop, gollop; gnash, and bite –
He can keep it up all night!
So I told him to his face
That he was a real disgrace.
Goodbye, Dad, goodbye, Mummy:
I'm writing this inside his tummy.

*President Reagan

Esquimau

Esquimau, esquimau,
Up to everywhere in snau!
On your little sledge you gau,
Leaping from ice flau to flau.
Now I knau, I knau, I knau
Why progress in the snau is slau!

A poemwem

One day, when I was in my prime,
I fell asleep on a railway lime.
Suddenly a girl came out of a forest:
I said, 'You must rhyme with florist.'
She said, 'No! I'm the spirit of romance!'
I said, 'Shall we dowance?'
She said, 'Do you fox-trot?'
I said, no, I could notrot.
She said, 'A waltz?'
I said, 'Of cowaltz!'

Pussy cat, pussy cat

Pussy cat, pussy cat,
Where have you been?
I went to London
To see the queen.
Pussy cat, pussy cat,
What did you see?
I saw a policeman
Following me.
Pussy cat, pussy cat,
What did he do?
He said to me,
'Home you go!
Shoo, shoo, shoo!'

The thin man

I know a man called Ranjit Singh:
He hardly ever wears a thing.
He is so thin it does appal,
And yet all day he shows it all.
It's not a sight I want to see –
Such thinness just depresses me.
He's got thin arms, he's got thin thighs –
My God, he's even got thin eyes!
You'd think a man as thin as that
Would wear boots, trousers,
   shirt and hat!

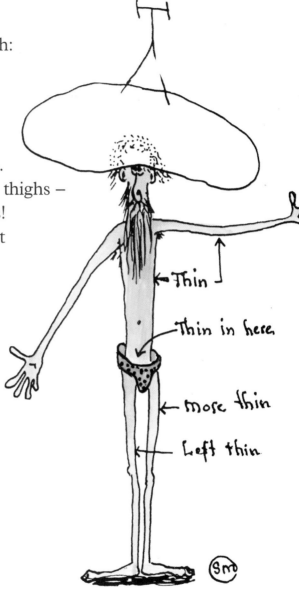

Fiddle faddle

Fiddle faddle
Fish fash
Flip flap flop
Diddle daddle
Dish dash
Clip clap clop
Fiddle diddle
Fish dish
Dish dash doo
Piddle diddle
Pish dish
Bim bam boo

My sister Kate

My sister Kate
Is *always* late.
But I'm
Always on time.

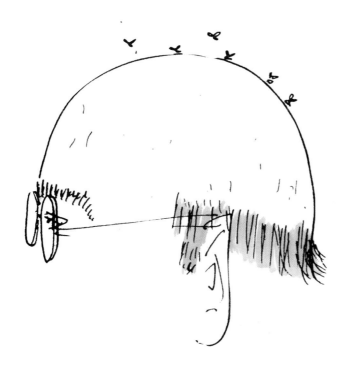

My granddad's old

My granddad's old
And lost his hair
And that's why flies
Are landing there.

So marched the Roman legion

SO MARCHED THE ROMAN LEGION
STRAIGHT DOWN WATLING STREET.
FOR MILES AROVND
THE ONLY SOVND
WAS THE TRAMP OF ROMAN FEET.

THEY WERE MARCHING ON LONDINIVM
TO PVT DOWN A REVOLT
BY BRITISH YOBS
AND BRITISH SLOBS,
ALL DRVNK ON HOPS AND MALT.

BVT WAITING IN LONDINIVM
WAS A LADY CHARIOTEER
WITH BLADES OF STEEL
STICKING OVT EACH WHEEL
AND HER NAME WAS BOVDICCA.

HER CHARIOTS CHARGED THE ROMANS,
WHO RAN AWAY IN FEAR,
SO THE BRITISH YOBS
AND THE BRITISH SLOBS
ALL WENT BACK ON THE BEER.

Nonsense II

Myrtle molled the Miller pole
While Tommy twigged the twoo
And Dolly dilled the dripper dole
As Willy wet the woo
Then Andy ate the Acker-cake
And Wendy wonged the groo
As Herbert hacked the matter rake.
And Bertha bonged the boo!
Then all together honged the hack
And widdle donkey doo
They pongled on the wally wall
And the time was half-past two.

Miller Pole   DRIPPER DOLE   ACKER CAKE   HATTER RAKE

Moo moo moo cow

Moo moo moo cow,
Mooing on the hill,
Moo moo moo cow,
Are you feeling ill?

Making all the mooing noise,
You must be in pain.
Moo moo moo moo,
There you go again!

Moo cow, moo cow,
Shall I call the vet?
Moo no, moo no,
Moo not yet:

Moo cow, moo cow,
Moo cow, it's not right –
Moo moo moo mooing
Mooing day and night.

Sad to think that moo cow
Moo cow mooing
Will end you up in a dinner pot
Stew stew stewing!

Crocodile

Croca croca crocodile
With a politician's smile
Showing all your massive teeth,
Just like Mr Edward Heath.
I bet my life if you could catch her
You would eat up Mrs Thatcher.
Perhaps you'd eat out the other menace
Mrs Thatcher's husband Denis.
For that Neil Kinnock would agree
To offer you the OBE.

Polar bear

Polar bear, polar bear,
How do you keep so clean?
You always seem to stay so white
No matter where you've been.

My mummy scrubs me every night
To wash the dirt away.
Somehow it all comes back again
When I go out and play.

Polar bear, polar bear,
Do you ever bath?
I seem to get so dirty
Just walking up the path.

I wish I was a polar bear,
So then every night
If someone tried to bath me,
I'd growl at them and bite!

Thylacine

Have you seen
The thylacine?
Or remotely where he's been?
People tell me by the score
They have seen the creature's spoor.
It used to live here in Tasmania
I'm certain that no more remain here.
The thylacine is surely linked
With other creatures now extinct!

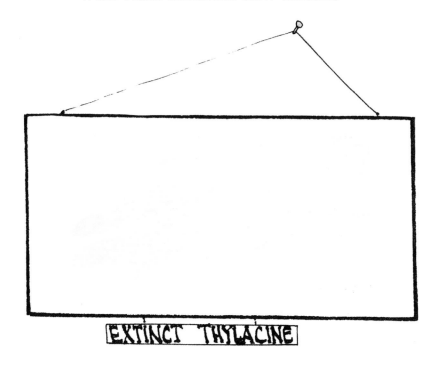

EXTINCT THYLACINE

Little Jim

Little Jim is very small.
He wanders up and down the hall.
Sometimes he wanders up the stairs
Or sits in one of daddy's chairs.
Sometimes we wonder where he's gone
And find him laying on the lawn.
He's very fond of chocolate bars.
He goes outside and watches stars.
Other times he's in the bath
Or wandering up the garden path.
He doesn't ever watch the telly –
Instead you find him eating jelly.
Little Jim talks very funny:
He has a nose that's always runny.
Sometimes he screams, sometimes he yells,
Sometimes he positively smells.
He walks around and sucks his thumb.
Sometimes he kicks me up the bum!
Still I treat him patiently
'Cos little Jim is only three.
Mum tells me he's my baby brother
Please God don't let her have another!

AB

A Bee!
A Bee!!
Is after me!!!
And that is why
I flee!!!!
I flee!!!!!
This bee
This bee
Appears to be
Very very
ANG
-ER
-REE

The bittern

I once saw a bittern
In the sky.
Why did that bittern
Fly so high?
Because once bittern,
Twice shy!

Pig-in-a-poke

Today I bought
A pig-in-a-poke.
Because of it
I'm stony-broke.
The poke I've bought's
Not very big,
But neither is
The piggy wig.
I've tried to get
The piggy out
By pulling at him
By the snout.
I pull *out*
But he pulls *in*!
Neither of us
Seems to win.
I've been pulling
For a year:
He hasn't budged
An inch I fear.
All the food

I give he's taken,
But so far
No sign of bacon.
I started pulling
At his tail
But even that
To no avail.
But then he gave
A grunt, a cough –
There and then
His tail came off!
And so goodbye
To you, my friend.
This piggy's tail
Has reached its end!

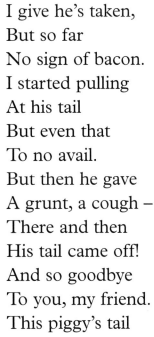

Hippety Hoppity

Hippety hoppity
Hoppity hoo
Goes the bounding
Kangeroo.
You can't lock him
In a pen
He would just
Leap out again.
It's hard to keep
Him in at all
For he can jump
A six-foot wall.
His leap is really
So immense
He can clear
A ten-foot fence.
You'd never keep him
In a zoo –
He'd just leap out
And over you.
No one so far
Has ever found a
Way to catch
The little bounder.
So, oh dear,
What can we do
To catch the bounding
Kangeroo?

Moral.
Never shoot a Kangeroo!
It's a nasty thing to do.
He won't harm me.
He won't harm you.
Hippety Happity Kangeroo!

Lord Lovington Ogden Rees

Lord Lovington Ogden Rees
Had a pair of knobbly knees
That shone like polished manganese.
And thus one of life's mysteries:
The sight of them caused some unease.
They looked like some new strange disease
Brought here by trading Goanese
Or sailors here from overseas
In weather minus ten degrees.
He fills them both with anti-freeze.
The only benefit he sees is
They take the shock, whenever he sneezes.

I've just been attacked

I've just been attacked
By wild bananas:
Oh, what shocking
Awful manas!
As I walked
Beneath their tree
A bunch of them
Jumped down on me.
Attacking a
Defenceless fellow,
As cowards go
They all were yellow.
I was saved
When from a tree
There came a hungry
Chim-pan-zee.
Then, in one great
Simian dive,
He skinned each one
Of them alive!
Even *then*
They weren't quite beaten
Until the last of
Them was eaten!

I met a Greek

I met a Greek
  Who wouldn't speak.

I met a Turk
  Who wouldn't work.

I met a Dane
  Who was insane.

I met a Scot
  Who just talked rot.

I met an Arab
  Who gave me a scarab.

I met a Swede
  Who couldn't read.

I met a German
  Who gave me ein sermon.

I met an Italian
  Who sold me a stallion.

I met an Eskimo
  With only one toe.

I met a Moroccan
  With only one sock on.

I met a Mongolian
  Who knew Napoleon.

I met a Croat
  Who had a sore throat.

I met a Sioux
  Who was six foot tioux.

I met a Spaniard
  Who sold me a lanyard.

I met a Slav
  Who made me lauv.

I met a Cambodian
  Who was a custodian.

I met a Majorcan
  Who wouldn't stop torcan.

I met a Fijian
  Who'd just done his knee in.

I met an Iraqi
  Who had a bad baqui.

Now with a Swiss
  I'm ending thiss.

It would be obscene

It would be obscene
For the Queen
To turn green.
It would be much more patriotic to
Turn red, white and blue.

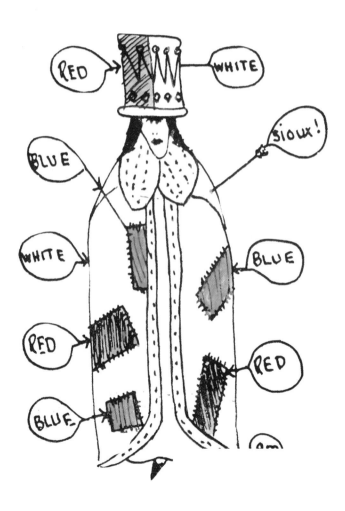

THE END